# University Teaching

*University Teaching: An introductory guide* is a vital tool for the new lecturer that aims to encourage and support an inquiry into university teaching and academic life. This book understands that teaching is not discrete but one of many activities integrated in academic work. It recognizes that teaching is directly affected by administrative concerns such as timetabling and workload demands, departmental culture, disciplinary research expectations and how we think about the purposes and values of higher education. The new lecturer must learn to adapt to and shape the circumstances of their academic work.

Understanding that teaching is an integral part of this work, rather than a dislocated discipline, can help us think about practice in new ways. Harland argues against the teaching–research divide and popular opinion that 'teaching takes time away from research'. He proffers the sentiment that all aspects of academic practice need to be considered when inquiring into learning how to teach, and that teaching is better understood when it is firmly embedded and integrated in this work. Writing from his experience extracted from a ten-year research project working with early career staff, he addresses popular concerns of academics, including:

- Lecturing
- Peer review of teaching
- Discussion as an approach to teaching
- Research and the new academic
- The subject and the idea of critical thinking

This clearly written and practical book will be ideal for all new lecturers in higher education, and also more seasoned academics wishing to progress their professional development.

**Tony Harland** is Associate Professor at the Higher Education Development Centre, University of Otago, New Zealand.

# University Teaching

An introductory guide

Tony Harland

Routledge
Taylor & Francis Group

LONDON AND NEW YORK

First published 2012
by Routledge
2 Park Square, Milton Park, Abingdon, Oxon OX14 4RN

Simultaneously published in the USA and Canada
by Routledge
711 Third Avenue, New York, NY 10017

*Routledge is an imprint of the Taylor & Francis Group, an informa business*

© 2012 Tony Harland

The right of Tony Harland to be identified as author of this work has been asserted by him in accordance with sections 77 and 78 of the Copyright, Designs and Patents Act 1988.

*British Library Cataloguing in Publication Data*
A catalogue record for this book is available from the British Library

*Library of Congress Cataloging in Publication Data*
A catalog record has been requested for this book

ISBN: 978-0-415-52430-8 (hbk)
ISBN: 978-0-415-52431-5 (pbk)
ISBN: 978-0-203-12060-6 (ebk)

Typeset in Galliard
by Taylor & Francis Books

For Sarah

# Contents

*List of figures*                                                      *viii*
*List of tables*                                                         *ix*
*Acknowledgements*                                                        *x*

Introduction                                                              1

1  Learning to teach in university                                       10

2  Peer review of teaching                                               23

3  Lecturing                                                             32

4  Discussion as an approach to teaching                                 46

5  Theory and practice in student learning                               58

6  Students past and present                                             68

7  Research and the new academic                                        77

8  Academic work                                                        84

9  The purposes and values of a university education                     95

10  The subject and the idea of critical thinking                      106

*Index*                                                                 *119*

# Figures

1.1  The Action Research Cycle                                        13
1.2  Forms of systematic inquiry                                      18
3.1  Engagement model for lecturing                                   43
4.1  Four objectives for discussion                                   48
4.2  A continuum of inquiry                                           52
5.1  Vygotsky's zone of proximal development                          63
10.1 Critical thinking quiz                                          107
10.2 A model for critical thinking as critical conscience            116

# Tables

1.1  The qualities of an inspirational teacher    14
1.2  Sources of primary data for evaluation and research into
university teaching    17
4.1  Workshop example (1)    50
4.2  Workshop example (2)    51
4.3  Techniques for questioning    53
6.1  Student approaches to a science project past and present    72
8.1  Problems with induction    88
9.1  The purposes of a university education    96
9.2  Students' ideas about negative and positive impacts of a
university education on society    97
10.1  Verbs for learning objectives derived from Bloom's
Taxonomy    111
10.2  Un-critical assessment    113
10.3  Extract from an interview with two second-year students
about assessment    115

# Acknowledgements

I would like to thank all the academics and students who have taken part in various research and development projects with me over the years. They gave their time generously and shared experiences of many important issues about academic life and teaching and learning in university. Without their care, thoughtful reflection and thorough analysis of ideas, this book could not have been written. Finally, I would like to thank Ayelet Cohen for her design for the book cover.

# Introduction

This book has been written for the new university lecturer to encourage and support an inquiry into university teaching and academic life. In the early months and years of a new lectureship there are various possibilities for academic work and the way a career plays out is contingent on how this work is understood and the choices made at the start.

It is primarily a book about learning to teach, but with teaching understood in the context of an academic practice, whatever that may entail for the individual. From working with new lecturers I have come to recognize 'teaching' is not discrete and that it is clearly an integral part of the various roles the university lecturer is expected to perform. For example, teaching is directly affected by administrative concerns such as timetabling and workload demands, departmental culture, expectations for disciplinary research and how we think about the purposes and values of academic work. Understanding the circumstances for teaching can help improve this practice.

When teaching is experienced as a disconnected part of work and professional formation, it seems to set itself against other activities, cause unnecessary tension and re-enforce the strongly held belief among new academics that there is a research–teaching divide. Sentiments such as 'teaching takes time away from research' are now quite common in the research-intensive university sector where teaching continues to be devalued because of the ascendency of research. My argument would be that most aspects of academic practice need to be considered in any inquiry into learning how to teach and that teaching is better understood when it is firmly embedded and integrated in this work.

The central topics within each chapter are written with such a perspective in mind. They were originally chosen after careful reflection on a ten-year project in which I worked each year with a new group of early career academics. The issues that were of concern to these academics form the core of the book. However, I have also included a chapter on the peer review of teaching, a topic rarely brought up by those with whom I colla- borated. I have done this because working alongside peers in the classroom is an option for professional learning that academics can use at any stage of their career. I argue that when peer review of teaching is done well, it can have a dramatic impact on teaching practice and student learning.

## The structure

I have organized the book for the individual reader and as a textbook to support an introductory programme on university teaching. The ten chapters provide the topics I would include in a typical semester-long introductory programme of postgraduate study for new lecturers. Each chapter provides a set of fundamental ideas and advice on an aspect of teaching and academic work. If used to support a series of seminars or workshop activities, this would be 'pre-reading'. I also include a section called 'Thoughts for reflection' that provides a range of ideas calculated to challenge thinking and promote further discussion. Some of these thoughts purposely present one side of an argument and they do not necessarily represent a value position I hold. They are included because they are relevant for the contemporary lecturer. After the references, there is a brief guide to further reading with particular reference to the classic books in higher education that I know have had a worldwide impact on academics, their teaching and academic life.

At the end of each chapter there is a passage from my research field notebook on topics that are close to, or complement, the chapter subject. These are presented on ruled paper in a handwritten font. Please think of these notes as narratives and interludes in the text or use them as a form of qualitative data as part of a personal inquiry into learning how to teach.

My overall strategy is to offer a text that recognizes knowledge must be modified as the individual figures out what will work in their unique practice situations and what suits their values. Although this approach suggests a highly individualized view of academic work, I also acknowledge that the academic community shares many common concerns. For example, there may be little similarity in the number of lectures required of each of us, but all academics share a concern about workloads. Similarly, our disciplinary knowledge may be the main determinant of much of our teaching, yet all university disciplines seem concerned about developing students as critical thinkers.

## Background to the research

I am currently employed as a higher education researcher working in academic development in a New Zealand university. My academic apprenticeship seems to be typical of the experiences of those I work with in my department. I did a first degree, a Masters by research and then a PhD (all in science – higher education research came later). At some point after my PhD I became good enough at research to obtain a position in a university that also included teaching and a myriad of other tasks for which I was not equipped. Some of these were administrative; others were related to a more mysterious idea termed 'service' or 'civic engagement'. Beyond research, I was unprepared for nearly all the requirements of my job. It struck me then that I was an impostor in many of my roles and also that this was a peculiar situation that would not occur in other professions.

Of course I rationalized this at the time by telling myself that I was learning on the job and also following a time-worn path for the academic profession. Years later I found that my early feelings of guilt and deception were shared by many of my colleagues, and I now understand this style of largely unsupported apprenticeship as potentially dangerous and definitely not ethical. I say this because of the negative impact the novice's lack of ability can have on their academic career and the learning experiences of countless generations of students.

Learning about academic work, including research, teaching and administration has traditionally played out in an *ad hoc*, trial-and-error fashion, often framed and guided by the rules of tenure and promotion and the opaque conventions of academia. Although such a strategy can work very well for some, for most it makes the attainment of competence and the journey to expert longer than it need be, and for everyone it reflects lost opportunities.

Yet, set against this apprenticeship model, is the relatively recent academic or educational development movement, focused primarily on supporting teaching through workshops, courses and other forms of support, such as mentoring schemes. All of these can guide and help new staff but, despite such change, learning to be an academic still contrasts markedly with other graduate occupations such as medicine and law in which the profession takes a great interest in the formation of their new members. For the PhD student who has completed a short period of research training, being called a 'university lecturer' without necessarily having the skills and knowledge to do this work, strikes me as rather strange, especially given the importance of higher education to students, society and the new knowledge economies.

## A note on academic practice

Although my main concern is university teaching, it is one task situated in an amalgam of complex work activities that can sometimes feel quite indistinct from each other. Although I have organized the chapters with topic headings that suggest what they are about, for example, research, teaching or learning, I reason that all the duties required of an academic need to be embedded and understood in a holistic account of academic life. It is this principle that is at the heart of this book.

Of course, we also partition our various functions and we do tend to experience these differently; there are times when we are giving a lecture and times when we are writing a research report. However, I argue that most of the activities we undertake are essential to each other and justify the broader concept of 'academic practice'. A close examination of academic work shows that the boundaries we experience between activities can be quite arbitrary. For example, when we supervise a postgraduate student, are we engaged in research or teaching? Are we teaching colleagues when we give a research seminar? When we collate student grades for an exam board are we teaching or is this administration? These issues should not be seen as semantic or trivial because higher education needs to address two important contemporary issues. The first is the undervaluing of teaching when compared to research and the second is the fragmentation experienced in contemporary academic life. In this book, I suggest that exploring the relationship between the various tasks expected of academics can help in re-evaluating teaching and alleviate some of the tension and pressure experienced from competing work activities.

There are, however, many paths to and within academia and recent attempts to make academic work more specialized has resulted in roles and responsibilities becoming much more diverse and harder to recognize. Teaching-only posts in the research-led universities are one example of this change, and academics with diverse backgrounds now find a place in our universities as the sector responds to different demands for its services. In my work, I find the main exception to entering a university with the more traditional PhD qualification is staff brought in for their professional knowledge and expertise in areas such as health science and commerce. In these cases, it could be argued that support needs are even greater than for the PhD entrant, as they may not even have research expertise to offer.

## Data sources

I have worked with new academic staff for the last 15 years and the ideas for this book were selected from the various concerns they have shared with me about their experiences of starting work at university. The primary data I draw on were collected over the last ten years of mentoring work with small groups of new staff at two universities (e.g. Staniforth & Harland, 2003). At monthly meetings during their first year, between 10 and 15 new academics from a variety of disciplines met to explore their experiences. The group discussions focused on identified needs with the aim of helping individuals acquire knowledge and information that was relevant, necessary and timely in their academic life. I learnt early on in this exercise that academic needs are distinctive because practices are situated in the unique context of a subject and department. Yet, there were also shared concerns that seemed to cross personal, disciplinary and social boundaries and these came up time and again. I have included these concerns in this book in an attempt to ensure that the topics are relevant to a broad academic community and I try to remain faithful to what my new colleagues wanted to know.

A lot of our conversations directly concerned students. Questions included: 'What were students expecting from their education?', 'How have they changed as learners in recent years?' and 'What standards are they capable of achieving?' I found that new academics assumed a lot about students and that on closer examination, assumptions often turned out to be false. To address this issue I have given students a voice and include the views of 24 alumni as they reflect on their experiences of university and explain how this equipped them for working life. Although Chapter 6 is about students, their reflections are also interspersed throughout other sections of the book.

Another key source of data comes from my observations of working as a peer reviewer in the lecture theatres and classrooms of over 200 of my academic colleagues. These data reflect a wide range of disciplines in four universities, and I also draw on video recordings of teaching, my field notes and written comments from academics and students about their experiences. I then revisit a number of studies I have done in the area of academic work and university teaching and include a small amount of interview data from a current unpublished project. Throughout I draw on established theories from the higher education field.

## Chapter 1: learning to teach in university

The subject of the first chapter is learning to teach in university. I suggest that what draws all academic work together is the notion of the 'academic as scholar' and that learning about teaching (or service or research) is best done through personal inquiry as a form of research. As most university lecturers have expertise in their disciplinary research area, I argue that they can turn such skills to learning about:

1  teaching;
2  all aspects of academic work for which they have not been prepared;
3  the relationship between the different aspects of academic work.

However, researching one's practice requires both an interest and time, and professional learning of this sort can sometimes be seen as just another competing activity in a packed working life. In many cases, academics would probably prefer a bit of advice that would sort out gaps in knowledge and quickly solve the problems they are encountering. So the chapter also includes suggestions for practice as well as some ideas for discussion and further inquiry.

## Chapter 2: peer review of teaching

I make a case in Chapter 2 that peer review of teaching is one of the best choices that an academic can make for their professional learning, with the caveat that it must be done well to warrant the investment in time. The chapter is very practical and provides a step-by-step guide to the peer review process (sometimes understood as teacher observation). My concern is with teachers working together for the purposes of learning and I do not deal with peer review of teaching as a summative process in which one colleague sits in judgement over another.

For those who are using this book as a text for a postgraduate programme, I suggest that peer review should be the foundation of the programme. The chapter has been included with this idea in mind. Course participants can learn from being reviewed or from being a reviewer. For all readers please consider working with a trusted colleague, give peer review of teaching a go and then judge its utility and worth.

## Chapter 3: lecturing

The majority of academics who invite me to review their teaching ask me to come to a lecture. The lecture continues to be extremely important in the contemporary university, both for student learning and as a principal teaching method. Learning how to give a lecture is a high priority for new staff.

I divide Chapter 3 into two parts. The first looks at the idea of the lecture and why we lecture, and the second at some practical ideas for the lecturer. Part one includes thoughts on how the lecture sits within a broader educational context, why the lecture is seen as an efficient teaching method and the idea of lecturing as performance. Part two provides advice and some simple strategies and theoretical concepts that seem to have wide appeal across different disciplines. I also discuss the impact of Power-Point, a visual aid that has been a topic of great interest to new university teachers. I end the chapter with a simple model focused on engaging lecturers and students in learning.

## Chapter 4: discussion as an approach to teaching

Learning through discussion is central to all education and in this chapter I suggest that academics consider discussion as an *approach* to teaching. So, rather than take a tutorial (or seminar or laboratory class, etc.) that will contain an element of discussion, discussion becomes the chosen method and main focus for teaching and student learning. The type of class becomes less relevant. Discussion is then a unifying concept that concerns all situations that bring students, or students and teachers, together to jointly construct learning through some form of exploratory discourse.

Discussion, however, is not just a method or technique, but a value commitment for teaching and learning in a certain way. It can take place in both formal and informal settings and can also be realized through highly structured curriculum activities. I argue that the key academic objection to using discussion, namely, student reluctance, can easily be overcome and some practical strategies for encouraging dialogue are provided.

## Chapter 5: theory and practice in student learning

I take an unusual and highly selective route through learning theory but justify this because the two ideas I present, although not equivalent in any sense, are those I have observed academics making intuitive connections with. Ease of connection or intuition may be a poor rationale for choice, however, I am also confident that for most academics, after coming across either idea, conceptions of the learner and teaching practice will change for the better.

The first theory is 'approaches to learning' in which set tasks drive very specific learning behaviours. As such the teacher can act in certain ways to control students. They can push them into taking either a deep or surface approach to their learning and this idea has been pre-eminent across higher education for the last four decades.

In contrast to the approaches to learning theory, there has also been great interest in constructivism and how students go about creating new knowledge and thinking. Here I introduce some established ideas from the field of educational psychology and in particular the work of Lev Vygotsky and Jerome Bruner.

## Chapter 6: students past and present

This chapter was included because of the many conversations I have had in which academics have assumed certain knowledge about students without having much evidence for their claims. Students don't like this; they can't do that; they have to have … and so on. When I have explored these beliefs with academics, I am repeatedly drawn to two contemporary ideas that are worth looking at. The first is that our new generation of university students are very different from those of the past. Such differences are typically related to technological changes in information and communication technology. The second idea is that the student studying in neoliberal times has a different connection to learning and their university experiences. Student attitudes are partly explained in terms of economic and social change and the impact this has on society and its institutions, including the university.

## Chapter 7: research and the new academic

Research is a fundamental part of academic life that is often singled out as the most prized of all activities. In New Zealand (where university academics are required in law to be researchers) and in the research-intensive institutions worldwide, status and rewards accrue to those who do well in research. As such, the new academic ignores this aspect of practice at a cost. Yet even when this is clearly understood, research is often put on hold during the early part of a career, usually because the immediate demands of teaching are more pressing. In this chapter I suggest a variety of ways of thinking about research activity and how it sits within a more holistic conception of academic practice.

## Chapter 8: academic work

With regard to academic work, I have selected two issues that have been repeatedly identified by new academics. The first is time management and the second concerns work allocation, in particular, what is a fair teaching load? Both issues could seem trivial but they play out in highly charged situations in which new staff members find themselves in disadvantaged positions as they attempt to become established in their department and university. There seems to be too much teaching asked of new lecturers and student numbers continue to expand (at least in the popular subjects) without increased resourcing. Who does this work becomes very important, especially when teaching takes academics away from research or when unbalanced teaching allocations are seen to be unfair. Those I collaborated with in the mentoring groups also had a healthy interest in workload allocations across the university and how their colleagues in different disciplines managed this aspect of academic life.

## Chapter 9: the purposes and values of a university education

Every new academic should ask what the purposes of a university education are and then question what their responsibility is in making sure these purposes are met. Each lecturer within an academic community is responsible for creating and disseminating knowledge, promoting higher learning (with its associated knowledge, skills and values), and acting as a gatekeeper for standards. These individual and collective undertakings give the university its unique place among societal institutions. If the academic community is serious about achieving higher educational outcomes with an array of specialized knowledge, skills and values, then they need to first understand the purposes of academic work. This task is highly complex and takes time to think through. However, it is just as big a challenge to align what we 'think' with what we 'do' and what we 'achieve'. Chapter 9 presents the views of various stakeholders on the purposes of a higher education.

## Chapter 10: the subject and the idea of critical thinking

If an academic compiled a list of what they thought were the purposes of a university education, then critical thinking is sure to be included. If the academic were then asked to prioritize their goals for teaching, then again critical thinking would be near the top of the list. We know that students come to university to take a degree in a subject of interest and that a higher education goes way beyond subject knowledge. The 'way beyond' can start with a consideration of critical thinking and I propose this concept should remain the first priority and continued focus for all university teachers, in all disciplines.

Because the idea of the student as a critical thinker is readily accepted almost universally in our academic communities, the concept is still foundational to the modern university. In this chapter I look at teaching and assessment in the context of critical thinking and take Barnett's theory of critical being (Barnett, 1997) and expand this to meet the requirements for university teaching in New Zealand and for Western liberal educational systems more generally.

## References

Barnett, R. (1997) *Higher education: A critical business*, Buckingham: The Society for Research into Higher Education and Open University Press.
Staniforth, D. & Harland, T. (2003) Reflection as practice: Collaborative action research for new academics, *Educational Action Research*, 11(1), 79–91.

# Chapter 1

# Learning to teach in university

## Introduction

New university lecturers are not usually formally trained for teaching nor are they expected to have a teaching qualification. They do, however, possess a wealth of knowledge about education and its practices. All lecturers have spent a good portion of their lives as students, know what it is like to be taught and so have many ideas and examples of what they like and don't like about teaching and learning. They remember their high-school teachers and university lecturers and know what was beneficial for them and also what did not help. This knowledge provides an idealized teaching model that can be a valuable starting position for learning to teach.

Personal experiences of being taught, however, are not enough in themselves. As they develop appropriate skills, lecturers also need to acknowledge the things they do well and what their limitations might be as they work out the full potential of teaching in practice. The new academic can reflect on images of teaching and try to model their disciplinary practices in this way; knowing what sorts of things they enjoyed and connecting teaching with the discipline and its particular knowledge forms. Past experiences must then become a part of an exercise in careful systematic reflection if these are to provide a more meaningful starting point for decisions about how and what to teach. This analytical process provides a useful foundation for practice and it is this type of personal inquiry professional programmes and workshops often support (in contrast to an expert telling academics what to do). The concept has many names and can be called researching one's practice, practitioner research or simply research into teaching. The focus is always on the subject of a teacher's learning.

A research approach to learning provides a level of academic and professional integrity and a clear strategy for the lecturer wishing to improve their craft, not just at the start but also throughout a career. New academics already have a measure of skill as researchers in their discipline and in this context are learners and knowledge creators. If they can think of their own teaching as a legitimate subject for study and use the same research skills to investigate this, then they create their own teaching knowledge.

An optimistic or idealistic view of the university might evoke an image of lecturers and students as learners at all times, in all activities, including research, service and teaching. Learning to teach in a university is about valuing the idea that teaching is an important component of academic work that merits and requires a similar investment in critical thought and action normally given to other parts of the job such as disciplinary research.

## The case for researching one's practice

Learning to teach in university is largely a process of trial and error as part of an informal academic apprenticeship. Institutions that offer professional development support provide short introductory or advanced postgraduate courses in teaching, and colleagues with more experience may provide help and advice. However, to a great extent teacher learning comes through carefully thinking about the experiences of practice. How did my class go today, what went well and what needs to change? These and similar questions are the mainstay of personal development and will remain so while university teaching is an individualistic and private activity.

It could be argued that trial and error has served universities well in the past and the potential of the lecturer to gradually build up expertise in this way should not be underestimated. However, this learning strategy tends to take considerable time and also limits what can be achieved. In our contemporary and complex, mass higher-education systems, for which society and most students pay considerable fees, there must be ethical concerns about how long it might take a lecturer to develop their teaching to an acceptable standard. A consequence of substandard teaching is that generations of university students receive a second-rate education while their teachers slowly improve. Should this be a concern to the profession, teaching development needs to start on day one of a new academic's appointment.

In contrast to teaching, most university lecturers, at least within the research-led university sector, have undergone years of research training to attain a reasonable level of research skills. For example, they know how to design projects, handle theory and make judgements about evidence. These skills have been learnt within their preferred subject but much of this expertise can be transferred into other areas of knowledge, such as studying teaching practice. Yet accepting that teaching, or more specifically 'one's own teaching', can be a subject for study, requires a shift in thinking for many academics.

The starting point for an inquiry into teaching may have roots in the introductory programmes universities offer new academics. Most courses I have come across are designed in a workshop mode with topics such as lecturing, small group teaching and assessment. Participants are asked to reflect on theory and connect new ideas to their own experiences and practice circumstances. These programmes are typically not discipline specific with lecturers from many fields taking part and sharing knowledge. Courses can, if done well, provide a positive start to a university career and also offer a foundation for further professional learning.

However, every lecturer's practice is constantly changing and for most, becoming a skilled teacher is a continuous undertaking. Lecturers teach distinctive subjects and in ways that are quite unique to the individual. Many have a great deal of freedom to determine what their students learn and the complexity and range of practice situations requires constant attention for every teacher. Using research skills appropriately for an inquiry into practice ensures that any learning is timely, relevant and useful for the individual.

If it is accepted that learning to teach can be done through research then it must share the same characteristics of any other form of research. If research is 'systematic inquiry made public' (Stenhouse, 1981), then research into teaching will be organized and methodical with practical decisions based on the best evidence and data available. A teacher's learning (the intended outcomes of a research inquiry) will be made known to peers in some way. Making this public provides an opportunity for the research and its claims to be reviewed. In doing so colleagues contribute to each other's learning.

The idea of learning about one's teaching practice through personal research has a long history that dates from the Action Research movement of the 1930s (Lewin, 1946) to more contemporary ideas about the Scholarship of Teaching and Learning (SoTL) (Boyer, 1990). Action Research is about identifying aspects of practice that need improving and then focusing on these through a systematic cycle of change, evaluation and then further change. Typically this activity will be action-orientated and focused on improving an identified problem:

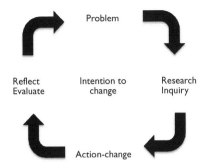

Problem

Reflect
Evaluate

Intention to
change

Research
Inquiry

Action-change

*Figure 1.1* The Action Research Cycle. A problem of practice is identified and this forms the basis of an inquiry. Action is taken after the results of the inquiry have been analysed and this is followed by an evaluation of the changes made. Any new problems are identified and these enter the next cycle of the Action Research project.

Action Research does not necessarily require a high level of research expertise and new academics without a strong background in disciplinary research can use it to change their practice. I would suggest that part of the inquiry process requires that published research and the theories of teaching are taken into account, and so skills in the critical review of primary and secondary sources of data are required to enhance the quality of the research cycle.

The Scholarship of Teaching and Learning (SoTL) came to prominence through the Carnegie Institute of America and its foremost advocate was Ernst Boyer (1990). Boyer brought the older medieval concept of the scholar up to date by suggesting that the idea of scholarship could be applied to all facets of our academic lives. The SoTL model proposes that we are scholars of research and so should be scholars of teaching. The values implicit in this work are congruent with my arguments for learning to teach by research. According to Boyer SoTL has four dimensions with the scholarship of:

1  discovery (creating new knowledge through discipline research);
2  integration (interpreting knowledge in and across the disciplines);
3  application (applying knowledge in service activities);
4  teaching (the study of teaching practice).

Boyer's model has, however, been seen as unnecessarily complex and poorly understood (Boshier, 2009). Being 'scholarly' in teaching and learning is a concept not easily defined and many academics do not seem to connect with SoTL, possibly because of embedded ideas about the nature of the structure of academic practice and how we experience this as either research, or teaching or service.

SoTL has certainly not attained the widespread adoption that Boyer might have hoped for, although it has generated much debate and seems to have been a catalyst for Carnegie's more recent promotion of the teacher as 'inquirer'. Learning to be a teacher through 'research into university teaching' can simplify SoTL, if it is accepted that practice can be the subject of research. However, Boyer also wanted to raise the status of teaching in relation to disciplinary research but I do not think new academics need be overanxious about such value differences. Disciplinary research tends to have a higher status than teaching and is rewarded as such (Chapter 7). Yet this simple fact of academic life should not rule out trying to become the best teacher possible.

## Sources of data

In any inquiry, whether or not it is Action Research, SoTL or a more general form of research into university teaching, there are similar steps in the process that include formulating a research question and gathering appropriate data. In addition, academics need to have some concept of what good teaching practice looks like.

The first exercise I give to new lecturers who take part in our introductory programmes is to ask individuals to think back to when they were students and identify one inspirational teacher. They then list that teacher's qualities and, importantly, explain why they think such qualities were significant to them as learners. I have repeated this exercise on numerous occasions and what new lecturers have to say is repeated time and again. They have strong feelings about what a quality teaching and learning experience is and they are also very aware that attaining this in practice is not straightforward. A typical list of attributes collated during a group exercise includes:

*Table 1.1* The qualities of an inspirational teacher: examples of responses collated between 2001 and 2010

| Characteristics of a good teacher | |
| --- | --- |
| High level of knowledge expertise | Well organized |
| Challenged thinking | Made it fun |
| Explained complex ideas | Respected an individual's knowledge |
| Knew each student | Showed humility |
| Creative | Listened to what students had to say |
| Enthusiastic | Showed genuine caring for |
| Sense of humour | student's learning |
| Strict but fair | Rewarded student's hard work |
| Engaging | Dedicated to discipline |
| Good communicator | |
| Good voice | |

Sometimes I hear ideas expressed in different ways. For example, one academic described a good teacher as someone 'you don't want to disappoint' and another said they needed to appear professional by 'wearing a suit'. However, at a certain level there is general agreement on 'what makes a good teacher' and these qualities can provide an excellent starting position from which to develop a deeper understanding of practice. Be aware that most of these academics recalled how they were taught, not what they were taught.

Although such characteristics may not be surprising, they lack detail and a context. An immediate reaction to such a list should be to ask a series of questions, for example:

- Which characteristics are more important?
- In what context do they work best?
- How are they related to each other?
- What really matters to students and/or teachers?
- How do they work in my subject?
- Do they have the same importance at first and third year?
- What are the limits of the teacher's responsibility?

The characteristics shown in Table 1.1 are also not equivalent with respect to how they might be acquired in professional life, because some are clearly personal attributes while others seem to be technical skills. Becoming a caring teacher when you are not necessarily a caring person might be more difficult than learning how to structure a class. Moreover, data showed that each inspirational teacher was highly unlikely to be seen in the same way by all the students in their class. What meets the needs of one does not necessarily meet the needs of another. Yet I see the same attributes proposed time and again in the exercise and they are mirrored in teaching and learning plans, mission statements and other documents concerning graduate attributes. There seems to be some general agreement about the broad characteristics of good teaching.

So what is it about being knowledgeable or being fair or listening to students that is important? Any answers need to be worked out over time by the individual teacher with respect to the knowledge of the discipline, the different contexts in which teaching takes place and the aims for student learning. While many new lecturers might like to be told how to teach, this is of limited use. More experienced teachers can pass on advice and tips but this will never substitute for treating one's own teaching as an ongoing inquiry. Asking how I can improve my understanding of (an aspect of practice) changes the nature of teaching and the teacher. My rationale for offering a list of the characteristics of good teaching is to provide a possible focus for an inquiry into a pertinent aspect of teaching. But this is not meant to limit research to seeking out what we know about good teaching – identifying pressing problems or particular areas of interest is likely to be a more relevant starting point. In any project, the researcher must first recognize a genuinely useful question focused on a particular part of practice, for example: How can I improve the level of student engagement? What does it mean to get to know each student? How can I improve assessment to reward the outcomes I am seeking? Why do students ask for the Power-Point slide handouts? Even seemingly small practical matters can quickly increase in complexity and interest once the inquiry is under way, and this will lead to new ways of thinking about teaching and provide new research challenges.

If it is to be critical, then research into teaching will nearly always rely on multiple sources of data and a wide range of evidence on which to base conclusions and direct action. In addition, like all research, the process will be systematic and take into consideration both established theories and other published accounts of practice. For those new to researching teaching it will be necessary to start with single issues and keep the project small and manageable, partly because this is good advice for researcher development, and partly because the new lecturer should be putting most of their time and effort into establishing their disciplinary research and teaching while they respond to all the other demands of academic work. Initially, time will be limited for teaching inquiry. For those in higher education institutions where disciplinary research is not a priority, then research into teaching can become more ambitious and more prominent in the early part of an academic career.

Nearly all types of practitioner research are completed within a qualitative framework and so require various data types. Teachers routinely evaluate their teaching and courses and the same data and collection methods can be adapted for research. Routine evaluation of teaching can also suggest questions for a well-designed research project. Common sources of data are shown in Table 1.2.

I have included practitioner research in the self-reflection dimension because analysis of qualitative data relies on researcher interpretation and research into practice is always individual in character. Reflecting on evaluation data can be a normal part of teaching and the outcomes may genuinely be adequate for developing practice. Being able to evaluate one's thinking is also an important and critical skill for professional learning. However, because all evaluation exercises tend to be private exercises and mainly involve only primary source data of a specific type, they may also be limiting. Typical methods for qualitative research include interviews, focus groups, surveys and document analysis. Importantly, there is also a wealth of theoretical knowledge that the new teacher can draw on as well as learning from the judgement and experiences of peers.

*Table 1.2* Sources of primary data for evaluation and research into university teaching. Sources are divided into four sections that rely on students, peer review (Chapter 2), self-evaluation and documentary evidence of student outcomes

| Sources of primary data | |
| --- | --- |
| *Student outcomes* | *Peer review* |
| Assessment (formative) | 1 Live |
| Grades (summative) | |
| Classroom assessment techniques[1] | • Classroom observation |
| Student work (projects, theses) | • Peer talks to students |
| Progression to postgraduate study | 2 Recorded |
| Progression to employment | |
| Employer feedback | • Video and audio |
| Rates of attrition | • Review of courses/materials |
| | 3 Reporting back |
| | Teaching awards and recognition |
| *Student perceptions* | *Self-evaluation* |
| Course evaluation (during or after) | Teaching journal |
| Teacher evaluation (after) | Field note book |
| Class representative feedback | Reflective course memo |
| Unsolicited feedback (e.g. email) | Portfolio |
| Student interviews | (all the above to include a philosophy |
| Focus groups | statement and meta-analysis) |
| Exit interviews | |
| Graduate opinion surveys | Practitioner research |
| External examiners | Research into university teaching |

[1] Angelo & Cross (1993).

## Disciplinary research and research into teaching

When academics consider research, they will naturally think about their subject and field of interest. If they take their research skills and develop a new subject (their own practice), they can also mirror what they are trying to achieve in their discipline and contribute to the established field of higher education. If the work is of sufficient quality, this type of research can be published in books and journal articles. It can then benefit a wider audience of educators and most disciplines have their own specialized teaching journals (e.g. *Journal of Geography in Higher Education, Medical Teacher*). There are also many publication possibilities in journals dedicated to the interdisciplinary field of higher education. Here we find academics whose primary research interest is higher education, publishing alongside academics for whom it is a secondary interest (Harland, 2009). The following diagram shows inquiry types currently used by university academics with outcomes that depend on intention, and the depth, scope and quality of the research inquiry. These form a hierarchy of knowledge forms as the teacher-researcher moves from private to pubic domains, and from careful reflections on practice to making a substantial contribution to the theories of higher education.

It may take many years to get to the stage of publishing the outcomes of teaching research in a journal, yet countless numbers of academics do this as part of their normal academic activities. The point of taking a research approach to learning about teaching is that each inquiry stage has value, from thinking about what happened in class today, reading a book chapter on education, doing a literature review or formulating a research question and designing a project. However, being committed to turning reflective practice or SoTL activities into published research can drive the academic to more sophisticated and critical levels of thinking and action. Many academics take a great deal of pleasure in researching aspects of their teaching and become very interested in teaching as a subject.

In promoting the idea of research into teaching I always think of this as a socially embedded practice and know that there is strength in the early

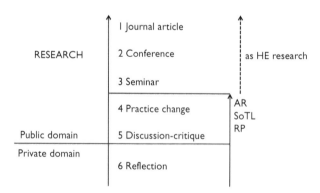

*Figure 1.2* Forms of systematic inquiry. A systematic inquiry becomes research when the outcomes are in the public domain. Typical examples are Action Research (AR), the Scholarship of Teaching and Learning (SoTL) and shared accounts of reflective practice (RP). Once we reach the stage of research seminars and journal articles, we enter the domain of Higher Education (HE) as a field of research.

career academic collaborating with others. Those taking a course in university teaching will probably be doing practice-focused projects of one sort or another and these are typically shared in a community. I tend not to think of the lone researcher that often characterizes the university academic.

In the broader context of academia, research into teaching chemistry or teaching history, for example, will not be valued as much as research into the subjects of chemistry or history (Becher, 1989). Research into teaching in a discipline, or in the field of higher education itself, tends to have low status in our academic communities, even when it is published in high-impact journals. This status situation need not be of concern. Being or becoming a researcher of teaching has great utility for developing practice:

> On the whole, within universities and among scholars, the status hierarchy in science attributes the highest status to basic research, secondary status to applied research, and virtually no status to formative and action research. The status hierarchy is reversed in real-world settings, where people with problems attribute the greatest significance to action and formative research that can help them solve their problems in a timely way and attach the least importance to basic research, which they consider remote and largely irrelevant to what they are doing on a day-to-day basis.
>
> Patton (2002, p. 223)

## Conclusion

It is essential to get teaching research under way as soon as possible while taking a long-term view of professional learning. If time is not allocated for this, it will soon be taken up by other activities and hard to reclaim. Because early career is characterized by competing demands, academics will need to partition time for learning about teaching so that it sits alongside all other aspects of academic work and a healthy work–life balance is achieved. I see both disciplinary research and research into teaching (or higher education more generally) as part of the competence of teaching: a good lecturer is a curious and skilled inquirer with concerns for becoming more knowledgeable and improving practice. If research into teaching is done in the spirit of critical inquiry, the new academic quickly gains in confidence. A good teacher will also wish to contribute knowledge to the wider community so the long-term view may be to produce inquiries that can be published in some form. Inquiry then becomes research in the field of higher education.

## Thoughts for reflection

1 Most university academics take up their first post without any formal training in teaching. I tend to think of a new career as the beginning of an academic apprenticeship. Academics are usually a little further along this apprenticeship route with their disciplinary research if they have undertaken a Masters or PhD. What would university teaching look like if all new academics were educated in research and teaching before they started in their first post? What if research and teacher education took place at the same time? (Harland, 2001). Such a case is made for other professions. You would not expect a doctor or lawyer or high-school teacher to start a fundamental aspect of their training after they began to practise.

2 My university, like most others in the Western tradition, assumes teaching expertise is limited for the new lecturer and support is now provided in the form of introductory and postgraduate courses, work-shops and mentoring. Nearly all this provision is voluntary so my institution also uses a form of tenure to assure a level of competence in teaching before a permanent lectureship is granted. What issues might be raised if research into teaching became a key part of an institution's reward structure?

3 There is some evidence that researching two subjects may benefit both (Harland, 2001). Those learning to be a disciplinary specialist change when they also have to think in another knowledge area with its own subject vocabulary, theoretical terms, epistemological foundations and social structures. How might the knowledge structure of the field of higher education impact on research in your first discipline?

## References

Angelo, T.A. & Cross, K.P. (1993) *Classroom assessment techniques: A handbook for college teachers*, 2nd edn, San Francisco: Jossey-Bass.

Becher, T. (1989) *Academic tribes and territories*, Buckingham: Open University Press.

Boshier, R. (2009) Why is the scholarship of teaching such a hard sell? *Higher Education Research and Development*, 28(1), 1–15.

Boyer, E.L. (1990) *Scholarship reconsidered: Priorities of the professoriate*, Princeton, NJ: The Carnegie Foundation for the Advancement of Teaching.

Harland, T. (2001) Pre-service teacher education for university lecturers: The academic apprentice, *Journal of Education for Teaching: International Research and Pedagogy*, 27(3), 269–76.

——(2009) People who study higher education, *Teaching in Higher Education*, 14(5), 579–82.

Lewin, K. (1946) Action research and minority problems, *Journal of Social Issues*, 2, 34–46.

Patton, M.Q. (2002) *Qualitative research and evaluation methods*, Thousand Oaks, CA: Sage Publications.

Stenhouse, L. (1981) What counts as research? *British Journal of Educational Studies*, 14(2), 103–14.

## Further reading

McNiff, J. (1993) *Teaching as learning: An action research approach*, London: Routledge.

# Field note 1
## Researching two subjects
-------------------------

I can't think of a better reason for becoming an academic than love of a subject (Rowland, 2006). If you don't love your subject, then it must be quite difficult coming into work each day. I am not even sure if this would be possible. Love is a strange term and the new academics I work with tend to describe their inspirational teacher as 'very knowledgeable' or as a 'subject expert'. But how do these experts come to know and what motivates and elevates them to such heights of knowledge expertise? It must be love of subject, or something close to this. In contrast, it seems to be the case that many students do not love what they are studying. Lewis Elton argues that it is the academic's 'task to interest students and enthuse them for our subject' (2000, p. 258) which, to my mind, is a rather contentious demand: 'Where is the student's freedom, responsibility and choice in this transaction?' Elton also points out that academics do not love all their subjects equally so why should we expect this of students?

Can the academic be as interested in the subject of 'themselves' as teachers? With research into teaching, one can make a move to separate 'self' from practice and also view theory as knowledge in application. In this sense, research into teaching is always viewed in the context of that teaching and its value judged by its value to practice. However, once university teaching is understood as the 'study of higher education', perhaps in geography or history or science, it then becomes much more like the subject of the academic's first disciplinary love. If disciplinary research is undertaken for the main purpose of becoming a better teacher, then any form of research into teaching will probably have a high value. If disciplinary research is valued in the context of 'knowledge for its own sake', then research into teaching is likely to be understood in a very different way. Furthermore, if the academic sees a clear separation between the activities of teaching and research, it is less likely that they will redirect their enthusiasm and disciplinary skills to know more about teaching. However, one way of achieving conceptual change is to financially reward academics who engage in teaching research although, without a genuine love of subject, one might wonder how this would differ from prostitution.

Elton, L. (2000) Turning academics into teachers: A discourse of love, Teaching in Higher Education, 5(2), 257–60.
Rowland, S. (2006) The enquiring university: Compliance and contestation in higher education, Maidenhead: Open University Press, McGraw-Hill Education.

# Chapter 2

# Peer review of teaching

## Introduction

Asking a colleague to come into your classroom or lecture theatre to help you investigate your teaching is without doubt one the best professional development choices you can make. There are some guiding principles for this type of collaboration that can help transform thinking and practice. The inquiry process is a joint exploration of what is happening in the classroom that aims to provide a foundation for further cycles of systematic critical reflection and change.

Unfortunately, the potential of working with a colleague to develop teaching practice is still poorly understood and those who do have ideas about what this entails tend to imagine being observed and assessed by someone with authority and responsibility for grading their teaching competence. What I propose is far removed from this stereotype and this chapter is written to encourage academics to open up their classrooms to others. However, if this practice is to become mainstream, it will also require university lecturers who are willing to step out of their comfort zone and take a risk as they expose their teaching to colleagues.

There are many terms for using another academic to help evaluate teaching but each conjures up a slightly different image. Three common expressions are:

1  peer observation;
2  peer supervision;
3  peer review.

The first suggests a teacher is being watched. The second implies something akin to supervision of postgraduate research students, or a clinical activity experienced in various health and therapeutic professions, and the third brings in other images from academia such as refereeing scholarly articles and research-grant applications. Peer observation seems to be the most common term but I favour the other two as they are more compatible with an inquiry method for professional learning and the values that I think should underpin the process. Because my institution has elected to use 'peer review', the name is familiar to me and I will stick with it throughout the chapter.

It is important to recognize two main ways of organizing peer review of teaching that depend on intended purpose. If the point of a review is to make summative judgements about the teacher or grade different facets of teaching activity, the process will contrast markedly to one that is only concerned with professional learning. The former is usually something 'done to' academics in order to help those who need to make decisions about competence, tenure and promotion. In these cases, the peer is normally a 'superior' peer (rather than an authentic peer) who is empowered to make the required assessment. The outcomes are always public.

The alternative is the development of learning and this type of peer review is usually done in a voluntary private partnership between academics of equal standing. In this case, the peer can have more or less expertise than the teacher. Of course, there will be some overlap between each type of peer review and those who engage in summative judgement will argue that the process also supports learning. However, the intention of each type of peer review results in very different experiences and outcomes.

I stress these points because in this chapter I am concerned only with professional learning and do not discuss peer review of teaching as a summative tool for making decisions about competence. I do argue, however, that evidence from non-summative peer review can be incorporated in statements about teaching quality in documents, such as teaching portfolios, and that these can be used as evidence of teaching quality for tenure and promotion.

## A guide to the peer review of teaching

I first suggest three key principles for consideration:

1  that the review is voluntary;
2  that the review is collaborative;
3  that the review is done for the purposes of professional learning.

Peer review of teaching involves partners working together to learn about each other's practice. It has the potential to offer critical insights into teaching that cannot be obtained through other evaluation methods. Peer review is based on mutual support between colleagues and can also work extremely well when it is done in partnership with a student.

Learning appears to emerge in three broad ways. First the peer has something from their experience or knowledge that they can pass on to the teacher. Second, learning develops from a joint exploration of what happened in the teaching session. Third, the review partners later reflect on the session and come to a new understanding of practice. There are five stages in the process:

## Stage 1: choosing an appropriate peer

The first and perhaps most important decision the teacher must make is the choice of reviewer. We are used to peer review of our research but this is generally 'blind'; however, there is no anonymity in the review of teaching and so it is essential that a peer relationship be established through mutual trust and respect. Exposing oneself to any kind of criticism can be quite daunting and if such a relationship is not possible, then the review will typically result in defensiveness inimical to learning. It is just as important, however, that the peer is prepared to be challenging and also open themselves to accepting criticism, otherwise the review risks warm and cosy affirmation that achieves little for either partner.

If a teacher's concerns have a curriculum focus, then they may seek collaboration with a reviewer from their own department or subject area. However, if the teacher is interested in more general issues of teaching and learning, then a peer from a different discipline can be chosen. I would suggest that this second strategy works best for most situations. Sharing interdisciplinary insights is both interesting and valuable and I have found that when a peer is from the teacher's department, they are often too close to bracket out embedded thoughts and feelings and often carry preconceptions of a colleague's practice. A little bit of distance seems to be a good thing.

## Stage 2: the initial briefing session

There are a number of decisions that should be negotiated before the review takes place. In order to develop a framework to guide the process both parties should be clear about the following:

- the aims and focus of the review;
- the way in which it will be conducted and the roles each will play.

In the briefing session it may be useful to begin by sharing some background details about the class being taught, for example its size, level, and the type of teaching method employed. The person initiating the review then carefully articulates what they are aiming to achieve in the class and then the proposed focus for the review. Identification of specific issues can be surprisingly difficult for those new to this and in the briefing session I am often presented with a general request 'I just want you to come and watch me teach'. However, it is preferable that clear guidance is given because this gives the reviewer an idea of issues significant to the teacher, and it also means the teacher is pressed into carefully reflecting on their practice, usually through thinking about what they feel they do well and what may need to change in some way. Previous course evaluations can suggest areas for exploration.

It is equally important that the aims and focus do not become so ambitious that they can't easily be achieved. A typical experience of mine is to be asked to sit in a lecture and observe students' learning. Surprisingly, it is possible to get some evidence of this but it is usually very limited. There may be better ways than peer review to find out about certain aspects of practice. When the focus point negotiations are done, ask if the teacher would like observations that fall outside the brief noted. This offer is usually welcomed but it may require tact, sensitivity and careful consideration as to how this information is used, if it all (see Stage 4).

The method for data collection should also be agreed as part of the brief. Some possible options include:

- live observation of classroom teaching with one peer watching the other;
- jointly examining recordings of classroom teaching (either video or audio);
- reviews of course materials;
- reporting back on classroom teaching: the peer is not present in the classroom (similar to clinical supervision);
- reporting back on courses and other curriculum matters.

If the process involves students (live or recorded observation of classes), then they need to be informed about the review. If the review is in a tutorial then decide in advance where the peer is to be seated and if notes should be taken (students and teachers can sometimes find this off-putting). Such issues are not so important for a lecture because the reviewer is fairly anonymous in a big group.

In more intimate teaching situations, students will think that either they or the lecturer are being assessed and this perception can alter what happens in the class. There is no easy way around this situation but I suggest to my colleagues that they introduce me as a 'collaborator in a teaching project' and then assure the class at the start that no assessment is involved. Despite this, students tend to be sceptical and they assume I am there to judge their teacher. On a number of occasions, I have been approached by students at the end of class who ask quietly, and in conspiratorial fashion; 'did he do alright?'

At the end of the briefing meeting decide when the debriefing session will take place (Stage 4 below) and make sure partners are satisfied with all aspects of the brief, including issues of confidentiality I believe to be unconditional.

### Reflecting on peer review

Peer review was good for our teaching because both me and my colleague trusted each other to keep it confidential. Whatever, we said to each other would not be used against us, and so it was in this environment that we could really discuss what portion of our course was of particular concern to us. I suppose it was like doctor/patient confidentiality.

In our sessions for peer review, we talked openly about what concerned us about our course. It was really good, 'cause I could open up about how incompetent I felt in one aspect of the course, and after a few laughs she gave me options for what I could do. I implemented one of the options, and immediately I saw good results. It was the confidentiality aspect of peer review and the trust that I had in my colleague and vice versa that made this system work for us.

## Stage 3: the review

The review itself constitutes the systematic collection of data that will be used in the debriefing session. The method of review influences data and this can come from multiple sources. For example, a peer may observe classroom teaching while the session is recorded on video. This strategy allows the peer to bring their insights from the live observation and the teacher to later view the video and stand back from their experiences as they revisit the session as a more detached observer.

## Stage 4: the debriefing session

Debriefing is aimed at constructive dialogue. The session may take place immediately after the review (which I tend to favour), but it can happen at a later stage or take the form of ongoing dialogue. Being critically constructive is an extremely important part of the exploration process but can also be difficult to achieve, especially for the novice reviewer. In addition, most teachers come out of a reviewed class wanting to know if their teaching is 'any good' and, because of this, some general acknowledgement of the positive aspects of the session needs to occur before discussions become more focused on the brief and issues for possible change.

If there are observations that fall outside the agreed framework great care is needed if these are brought into the conversation. As a rule it is better not to cross boundaries, but on technical issues (as opposed to observations of a personal nature) there may be little at risk and advice is normally welcome. The debriefing session is not the place to bring up the possibility of extending the original agreement, however, additional ideas generated *during* discussions are an essential part of a joint investigation into professional learning. A peer reviewer is not there to tell someone how to teach, or to say how he or she teaches, but rather to explore teaching in a form of a mutual inquiry.

## Stage 5: critical reflection

Peer review of teaching provides an opportunity for reciprocal learning for the teacher and peer. After the debriefing session it is important for each to consider:

- What has been learnt from the review?
- What action will be taken as a result of the review?
- What changes will be made to the review process for the future?

Reflective writing is a way of consolidating ideas, generating new thinking and providing a permanent record of the experience. Either party can write a summary of the outcomes and these accounts can be shared or kept private. Learning and changes to practice that result from peer review can be included in reflective statements in teaching portfolios as evaluative evidence. These can be an important part of making a case for teaching quality (for examples see Seldin *et al.*, 2010).

Mastering the review process is challenging and partners can learn over time the best way to help each other. Typically two academics enter a reciprocal agreement and each takes a turn at being reviewed. Another way of finding out about peer review of teaching is to accompany an experienced reviewer and see how they do it. This apprenticeship approach can lead to a review triad with three colleagues collaborating and learning from each other.

## Summary

| Stage | Activity |
|---|---|
| 1 | Choosing an appropriate peer |
| 2 | The initial briefing session |
| 3 | The review |
| 4 | The debriefing session |
| 5 | Critical reflection |

Peer review of teaching to support learning is a highly structured inquiry process that allows peers to gain insights into practice that are difficult to obtain through other evaluative methods. Although I have offered best practice guidelines, peers should be prepared to explore the method as they gain experience and come to their own understanding of peer review's benefits and limitations.

Peer review can change a teacher's perceptions about practice and help with their self-esteem, and these effects are immediate. I have never taken part in peer review without the unexpected happening and learning something quite new. The process, when done for evaluation and learning, rather than judgement and grading, has the potential to reveal unexplored thoughts and ideas. It opens up one's classroom to colleagues and new relationships develop that are reciprocal in nature. Even when it is done in confidence and for the purposes of professional learning, the outcomes and changes to practice can be documented and included in formal appraisals where evidence of teaching quality is required.

## Thoughts for reflection

1  Peer review can be a powerful tool for the new lecturer as part of an inquiry into teaching but it requires an investment in time. A briefing–review–debriefing can take three hours or more and not all academics want to invest this amount of time. How often someone needs to use peer review is open but there may be a point where, if it is repeated too often, the benefits may start to diminish. I would suggest that every new teacher gives it a try, and if it is seen to be useful or have potential, think about it again but only when a problem requires attention or the academic feels they are in a rut and requires some help to change or refresh practice.

2  Teaching is a complex practical activity and, although we can learn from reading, discussing and sharing ideas, we should never ignore the chance of inquiring into experiences. Peer review as a joint inquiry can be seen as a type of collaborative Action Research. When we team-teach, how could our normal and established collaborative activities be turned into a form of peer review?

3  Who you get to review your teaching is important and this can be anyone including an undergraduate student, a postgraduate, a new lecturer or an experienced lecturer. What might the difference be in each of these cases?

4  Peer review can be undertaken with someone from your subject area or from another field entirely. I once had a very successful experience working with a law lecturer teaching French Law using only the French

language in class (my background is science and higher education, my French is poor and my knowledge of French legal terms and concepts non-existent). What might explain the success of this peer review?

5  Peer review of research articles and grant proposals are usually done anonymously. What would constitute a good educational case for the anonymous peer review of teaching?

## References

Seldin, P., Miller, J.E., Seldin, C.A. & McKeachie, W. (2010) *The teaching portfolio: A practical guide to improved performance and promotion/tenure decisions*, 4th edn, San Francisco: Jossey-Bass.

## Further reading

Brookfield, S.D. (1995) *Becoming a critically reflective teacher*, San Francisco: Jossey-Bass.
Schön, D. (1987) *Educating the reflective practitioner*, London: Jossey-Bass.

# Field note 2
## How I work with peer review
- - - - - - - - - - - - - - - - - - - - - - - -

When I observe a colleague teaching I create a minute-by-minute description of what is happening in the session. I jot down everything that is happening, however mundane it might seem.

8.58   Students streaming into the lecture, picking up handout on the way in. Some seem to forget to do this and turn back when they realize, creating a log-jam of students
8.59   Opening PowerPoint slide is up now and two students are wanting to talk to the lecturer
9.00   Lecturer talking to the two students
9.01   Late students arriving through the other door and no handouts available on that side of the lecture theatre
9.02   Lecture starts, students still settling and talking. Late arrival looks embarrassed
9.03   and so on ... for 47 minutes

During this process, when an event occurs that may have some bearing on the issues that I have been asked to focus on, I note my thoughts down. Whenever something occurs outside this brief, I also write this down if I think it might be important. I mark each of these observations in a different way.

When we debrief, I simply read through my time-diary, pausing at the end of each observation. What then happens is that my colleague will respond and a conversation develops around a point of practice. The entire debrief is structured by the written time-diary.

When we come to explore issues raised in the briefing, I try to give these more thought and time. Whether or not I decide to raise issues that were outside the brief is a more difficult decision and requires fine judgement. On balance, I feel that it is best to have this option because it is not always possible to predict and plan for everything in advance of a teaching session. It is also surprising how often a small piece of advice can make an important difference. In the example above, it was a better way to ensure all students got a handout in a timely way.

# Chapter 3

# Lecturing

## Introduction

The lecture continues to be important in the modern university, despite consistent reports that it is an anachronism from a bygone age. It is a method of teaching that attracts a lot of debate, and opinions about the educational effectiveness of the lecture are often polarized. There are those who are very keen to see the lecture disappear altogether and others who have a strong wish to see it preserved or enhanced. I have a suspicion that what underpins most arguments are the past experiences of sitting through lectures that were either enjoyed or endured. However, despite different views, lectures will remain central to the experiences of students for the foreseeable future simply because of the embedded teaching structures and organization found in nearly all universities. Yet for this experience to be valued by academics and students, it is important for both parties to understand the educational rationale for lecturing.

In this chapter, I would like to address lecturing in a way that helps the new academic explore some of the contemporary thinking around this form of teaching. I start from the position that we are well aware that lectures can be good for student learning (even if they do not always achieve this), they provide for teaching with economies of scale and they are culturally embedded in our institutions. What I then focus on are the problems and challenges that new academics encounter when they first start lecturing. The chapter is in two main parts:

### Part I: ideas about the contemporary lecture

In this section I explore three conceptual ideas about the lecture that I have found to be of interest to new academics. These ideas emerged in discussions within the mentoring support groups between 2002 and 2009. I end this section with some thoughts on why we lecture in the first place.

*Part 2: the easily learnt lesson*

In this section I present a few simple and practical ideas that may be worth implementing in practice. In doing so, I only include what I think has currency across different disciplinary contexts and what might work for a range of individuals. For those looking for a more extensive account of 'how to' lecture, then Donald Bligh's seminal work *What's the use of lectures?* needs a home on your bookshelf. It was first published in 1972 with a more recent revised edition (Bligh, 1998).

## Part 1: ideas about the contemporary lecture

### Lectures never stand outside a broader educational context

This point may appear obvious but it needs to be reiterated because giving lectures seems to eclipse other teaching or learning tasks for those new to university teaching. The lecture can achieve certain things but not others and so this mode of teaching sits within a broader educational context in which the student will experience many different teaching and learning approaches. At times, lectures seem to frame the entire university experience but by themselves they are highly unlikely to achieve the outcomes we desire of our graduates. The lecture only succeeds alongside other formal and informal educational experiences including independent work, inquiry tasks, tutorial discussion, laboratories, opportunities to practise skills and so on. Lectures are significant in the minds of most academics and students but are not sufficient for a higher education. It is therefore incumbent on the lecturer to find out and understand how their lectures integrate within the overall student learning experience.

### Lectures are efficient

It is often claimed that lectures are an 'efficient' way of teaching because we usually lecture to large numbers of students at the same time. However, this shared experience is also unique and has implications for the student and lecturer that go way beyond the idea of organizing and providing knowledge for lots of people. If we put knowledge as information to one side, each lecturer can then carefully reflect on the criteria they would use to judge efficiency. Here are two questions that might help in this task: First, what can reasonably be achieved as an outcome for student learning and, second, how can students be taught as a large social group and respected as individual learners? Please speak to experienced lecturers in your discipline and explore these challenges to find out what they have to say about them, what they are trying to achieve, and also what they think, in addition to the planned outcomes, might be happening in their lectures. There are no easy answers.

### The lecture and performance

I have found that performance is the biggest concern for most new lecturers. They frequently express anxiety about walking into a lecture theatre and communicating with a large audience, and intuitively understand that they will be performing in a lecture 'theatre' and on 'stage'. I recognize that there is concern, especially among some educational experts, that the lecture could consist of no more than performance and this is worrying, especially if it really is just entertainment and there are no reasonable educational outcomes. However, if such shallow performances do exist it is likely that students would soon tire of them, make their voices heard and make better use of their time.

I can, however, see why lecturers need to have some form of entertainment in mind as a precondition for engaging their audience. Lecturers require some stage presence, a good speaking voice and a story that keeps the audience's attention. Again, such ideas could be seen to represent an anti-educational position but without this we risk boredom, inattentiveness and lack of engagement on the part of the learner. By far the most common responses I get from students about the lecture they have just experienced is that it was either 'OK' or 'boring' and this observation reflects a study by Mann and Robinson (2009) who surveyed 211 students across a university and found that 59 per cent thought their lectures boring half the time and 30 per cent boring most of the time. For someone like myself who has a strong value for lecturing, such responses are disheartening because 'boredom' and 'learning' seem incompatible when they occur together.

Consider also that a good stage actor has a deep respect for their audience and that this is a defining value for the art. A well-told story is necessary and an actor and audience who do not intimately and emotionally connect will feel unfulfilled. Similarly, a good lecturer performing to students will show consideration for their learning experiences, recognize the narrative character of the lecturing method and treat the occasion as a shared experience. The challenge is to make the lecture engaging so that it can be educational. For some, such a performance is easy and for others, the subject seems to take care of these issues. I learnt early in my career that Zoology students enjoy hearing about dolphins and whales but are generally much less interested in non-parametric statistics. Yet if you are disadvantaged by your subject but enthusiastic, passionate or show a genuine interest in the topic (and also care about teaching) students will generally respond to your lectures positively (see Kane et al., 2004).

Most of us will never be charismatic performers and each lecturer is unique in style and preferences. However, to neglect the performance element of lecturing is costly. If you feel that you can't cultivate some dimension of performance, or that your subject is inherently difficult to script in a captivating way, then you need to structure your lecture very carefully to get by and I will come back to this idea in Part 2 of the chapter.

### What determines our decisions to lecture?

I have not heard the 'why' question asked by those at an early stage of their career but feel that it is important to explore some of the reasons why we lecture because institutions seem to use the method too often. I am sure that if university lecturers were free to teach in any way they wished, with class sizes of their choice, the lecture would gradually become an uncommon event, possibly analogous to the occasional research seminar. I have worked with many lecturers and nearly all find that to provide a series of well-thought-out lectures, and do them well, is a huge task and challenge. The preparation time alone creates stress because it competes with other pressing work commitments.

I recently took a close look at my current institution and came up with a list of the key determinants that drive the new academic to use this mode of teaching. These may play out in similar fashion in other universities:

1  My university's modular system emphasizes flexibility and choice for its 20,000 or so students. There are relatively few core compulsory courses (outside professional subjects like medicine). Lectures therefore need to be carefully timetabled and each lecturer who joins an established programme is typically given a number of slots they need to fill. If you teach module X in subject Y, you lecture 11–12 noon on a Tuesday and Thursday for 12 weeks. And you find that this has been going on for years. These circumstances have evolved over time, do not seem to be questioned and change only when there are major curriculum reviews that temporarily jolt an immensely complex timetabling system that quickly re-adjusts. When courses are stable, the main determinant of why we give lectures seems to be the historic nature of the timetable.

2  The second driver is the expectations of students and academics. Students paying substantial amounts of money for their degree expect to receive lectures in return and so we give our 'customers' what they want. Academics, on the other hand, are expected to have equal workloads and a proxy measure for a teaching workload is the number of lectures given. On occasion, there may be good pedagogical reasons for giving fewer lectures but when I have suggested this to colleagues, I am usually told

that if they cut any, they will be criticized for not doing their fair share of teaching.

3   Another, but more-subtle determinant, is the new technology of learning management systems. These are coupled tightly to the lecture thus re-enforcing our rationale for lecturing. At my university, we have a single management system that standardizes student and lecturer experiences across the institution and its main use is a repository of lecture notes and PowerPoint slides. Students like this type of information to be available online. Naturally the system is also used for course management but its full potential and functionality, for example online discussion, is much less common.

4   Then there are the dedicated physical spaces and the tiered lecture theatres that lend themselves to the lecture method and either exclude or make difficult other forms of teaching.

It is a sobering thought that timetables, student demands, workload tensions and physical and virtual spaces could be the main determinants of why we lecture. Ultimately, it seems many academics have little choice in this matter and simply get on with the job.

## Part 2: the easily learnt lesson

When I work with new or experienced academics on lecturing they seek tips, advice and practical ideas at some point in our conversations. Like their students, the easily learnt lesson is an attractive idea. But I am also convinced that there is very little benefit to be had in the 'Ten steps to successful lecturing' approach. Of course, academics are prepared to embark on the harder-learnt lessons, but they still have an expectation that is, in my view, reasonable, that there is knowledge about lecturing that can be passed on to the novice by those with more experience. However, difficulties in doing this arise because no two lecturers are the same and what suits one may not be relevant to another. The student cohort also changes constantly and the discipline and subject dictates much of what can happen in a lecture. Bearing these caveats in mind, the following sections contain some general observations and advice that seem to have wide applicability across a range of disciplines.

### Break it up

The best practical advice I have on planning and organizing a lecture is to break it up into a small number of parts. This strategy is a general principle that works – most of the time. In true narrative style, have a beginning, middle and end and then ensure the middle is done in two or three sections that contain *differences* of some sort. It does not seem to matter what form knowledge is presented in, what the learning objectives are or what lecturing style is preferred. The point is to move from one 'activity' to another for example, moving from a linear exposition of knowledge to applying this to a problem. Or, from students making lecture notes to sitting back and observing a series of illustrations. Whatever the change, the variations seem to be positive for student experiences and learning.

There is some theoretical evidence to support this idea. Bligh (1998) presents cases from psychology that suggest after 15–20 minutes of continuous activity a learner's attention can start to wane. It therefore seems reasonable as a theory to have a disrupted structure with clear transitions that ensure students remain attentive to what you wish to communicate, and that this will enable your audience to stay with you for the full 50 minutes. Three parts typically provide enough difference and moving from one to another signals the change. Structure and organization are likely to be an even more important consideration for the lecturer who is not such an accomplished performer, or has a difficult topic to teach or who teaches on a compulsory service-type course with less-than enthusiastic students.

### The advance organizer

It has been suggested that students should know what is coming up in the lecture in such a way that it allows them to connect with what they already know and can do. For Ausubel (1968), this is the most important determinant of student learning. What I see lecturers do most often in this respect is to briefly recap on what was supposed to have been learnt in the previous lecture, and then signal what is to come. The students are then orientated to their learning and expectations for the forthcoming lecture. Yet this strategy only touches on what Ausubel is suggesting:

> If I had to reduce all of educational psychology to just one principle, I would say this: the most important single factor influencing learning is what the learner already knows. Ascertain this and teach him accordingly.
> (Ausubel, 1968, p. vi)

A major concern with this principle, and lecturing more generally, is that we more or less assume that all the students sitting in front of us are starting from the same point and that they are learning at the same rate and in the same way. This situation reflects the hardest challenge facing any academic: how to determine the correct level to pitch a lecture, how to work out how this changes for first, second, or third years, and how to teach all students (the brightest, those who struggle and everyone in between).

Teaching all students will always be an aspiration because there are such varied backgrounds within the student cohort, and capabilities and individual attitudes towards learning will constantly fluctuate. Although a lecturer seldom meets all needs in such an environment, it is still a worthy goal. The biggest risk seems to be in lowering standards as an easy option for meeting majority needs. To help with this challenge, run your lectures past a more experienced colleague.

I would also take Ausubel's ideas further by asking the lecturer to find out who their learners are. Lecturing to students with whom you have some relationship is very different from lecturing to an anonymous group. Getting to know students in the lecture theatre is difficult but this can be done in other ways, for example, through taking on roles such as course advising and tutorial or laboratory teaching. If lecturers (or their institutions acting on their behalf) give this type of work to part-time teachers or postgraduate tutors (an increasingly common strategy to save money) they relinquish a valuable opportunity for getting together with their students and so better understand them as learners.

### Classroom assessment techniques

Classroom assessment techniques (CATs) were proposed by Tom Angelo and Pat Cross (Angelo & Cross, 1993). CATs can provide quick evaluative information about student learning and are simple to use. For example, near the end of a lecture ask students to jot down an answer to two questions:

1   What is the most important thing I learnt from this lecture?
2   What still puzzles me?

Ask them to drop their answers in a box on the way out of the lecture theatre and you have a set of anonymous responses to what you have just taught. At the start of the next lecture, let the students know what the class response was and how your teaching has been modified (or not) to take into account their responses. There are many variations of CATs and because of the small amount of time required to deploy them they are sometimes called 'minute papers' (although two to three minutes is usually required). Give out the CAT towards the end of the lecture. I have found that doing it at the very end is bad timing because students switch off and are thinking more about their move to the next class.

### Lectures are a good place to sit and listen

An experienced professor said to me that if students were attentive and actively engaged in all their lectures, tutorials, laboratories and independent projects, most would burn out quickly and none would last a semester. There is only so much critical engagement a student can commit to and a limit to reserves of mental energy. I think of this idea as 'learning saturation' and it is one reason why terms and semesters need to be reasonably short and why students (especially those who are highly dedicated and always want to do the best they can) need their long breaks and holidays to rest and recover. Remember that most students will also have commitments outside university during term time, such as employment or looking after a family.

So we should be aware that in any lecture, there will be those who need to relax from time to time and others who simply enjoy sitting down and listening to what is on offer. As such, the idea of incorporating active learning activities in a lecture may have educational potential, but should be used in a measured way in this format. Lectures are mainly about knowledge organization, explaining difficult concepts and theories and offering an experienced synthesis of ideas to students. Other active forms of learning are usually better suited to different teaching situations, such as tutorials or research projects. The lecture does not have to fulfil all our desires for student outcomes and should be used for what it does best. That is not to say we can't have students actively engaged in knowledge production or in critical thinking, just that we need to include active learning tasks with good justification, when we do use them, not expect too much of students. Some lecturers see activity as a way of control to ensure that those who attend are there in mind as well as body. If we accept the idea of lecturing as performance, a successful lecturer will invite and draw students into their world and field of inquiry, without the need to directly command the audience.

### PowerPoint

For better or worse, presentations in lecturing, seminars and conferences, have been colonized by PowerPoint. This digital tool also seems to be the preferred method for organizing lecture material and all but two of the hundreds of lecturers I have observed in recent years used PowerPoint for both writing and presenting their lectures. I realize that there are various digital presentational tools available to the academic but PowerPoint has become the common term, so I use it in this general sense.

It seems relatively easy to organize and structure thinking and knowledge with the aid of PowerPoint, and so there is the bonus of having the lecture presentation completed at the same time as the planning. PowerPoint slides can also act as a support for the novice and for those who need to overcome nervousness, lack of confidence and expertise. Students also like to have the slide handouts to annotate during the lecture or be able to access them later in digital form on a learning management system. These handouts come to represent the heart of the curriculum in the students' minds, even when the lecturer understands the lecture and handout as part of a wider learning experience. I have heard more than one colleague say that students who 'have the slides' think they possess enough knowledge to get through the course. For some, PowerPoint slide handouts are a proxy for what is required of a higher education.

I commonly see students collecting the handouts as they enter the lecture theatre and then, as the lecture progresses, annotate or add information to these. Of concern is that the attenuated information on the slides can make little sense on its own and when students look back on these, even with their additional notes, they are insufficient to ensure genuine under-standing. Of course, such a situation may encourage students to relearn the lecture material in other ways.

Another observation is that the skill of note taking in the more traditional oral lecture of pre-PowerPoint times seems to be uncommon. If this is true across higher education more generally, then we are losing a technique for student learning. Writing, when experienced as a way of 'learning to think', has long been recognized as supporting the critical traditions of a higher education. If it no longer happens through lecture theatre note taking and re-editing, then it needs to happen in other places or in some other form.

Students may like PowerPoint and the handouts but they also report that presentation after presentation is 'clearly boredom-inducing' (Mann & Robinson, 2009, p. 255). So they, like their lecturers, are torn: they want PowerPoint to make learning easy but they also recognize that their preferences result in a more tedious university experience. We have ended up in a remarkable situation in which lecturers and students are attracted and repulsed by this technology.

The jury is out regarding the impact of PowerPoint and after nearly 30 years of use, there is little empirical evidence (either quantitative or qualitative) on the influence of PowerPoint on student thinking and learning. The seminal work of Edward Tufte is a rare exception (Tufte, 2003). Tufte carried out a linguistic analysis of different communication strategies in NASA prior to the Columbia space shuttle disaster. He suggested that attenuation of more complex information when PowerPoint was used led to incomplete understanding and different decision-making when compared to other forms of digital communication, such as email. Tufte has also been associated with the phrase 'PowerPoint Poisoning'.

There are, in contrast, many published accounts concerning PowerPoint based on stories of experience, intuition or a particular value position. These express a range of ideas that argue for or against this learning

technology. I would suggest that the only conclusion we can safe¹
the present time is that we really do not know what we are doing to success.
generations of students by organizing our lectures with this tool. Academia is
certainly getting more creative with PowerPoint and everything we do
with it seems high-impact, slick and professional. But as Marshall McLuhan
pointed out in the 1960s, 'the medium is the message' and the sooner we
understand the medium of PowerPoint in our lectures, the better.

My concern for the new lecturer is that PowerPoint instantly captures
practice. For the beginner, it is very easy to construct and deliver a lecture
using this medium, however, the longer this practice goes on, the harder it
is to step outside of it and seriously consider other possibilities. So we have
ended up with students and lecturers being aware of the benefits and costs
of digital representation technology. I think of PowerPoint lecturing as
addictive in some way because, as time passes, withdrawal becomes more
difficult. Perhaps we need a pharmaceutical-type disclaimer for such digital
media: 'use with caution'.

### The lecture as an educational experiment

The concept of 'teaching as an experiment' has much to commend it
generally, but the idea has immediate currency in the lecturing context
where the academic has a large amount of control over what happens in
the 50 minutes of each class. Simple evaluative data (e.g. CATs) on the
impact of what is happening can easily be gathered and then the lecturer
can systematically make small alterations and test these to see how they
work from class to class. Having observed one or two spectacular failures
around radical transformation, I would always recommend minor and
incremental change to minimize risk, but also ensure risk-taking remains
on the agenda. It takes time to learn how to lecture, work out what we want
to achieve and what we are capable of. If ideas are introduced gradually, they
will probably suit the lecturer's developing skills and personality and in this
way remain authentic. You can always tell when lecturing is forced as it
tends to appear artificial and amateur.

Data gathering is an important part of any experiment and the success
or otherwise of new ways of working need to be based on some form of
evidence. Intuition may not be enough and a sensible starting point for
evaluation is listening to students and what they think about their experiences.
However, collaborating with peers can also provide a different perspective
and, as discussed in Chapter 2, the time taken for peer review can be well
worth the effort.

And one last word of advice: don't tell the students you are trying something
new. As an academic developer I am often asked to review a new classroom

innovation and provide some peer comments. I have observed that lecturers feel the need to be confessional or 'upfront' about the changes they are about to introduce and this is usually counterproductive and unsettling for students. In most cases, they were not expecting any alternative and signalling a new practice focuses them on the lecturer, teaching methods and change, rather than what needs to be learnt. Similarly, since I stopped using the label 'Problem-based learning' (PBL), I have had much more success using this (now unnamed) educational inquiry technique. I used to tell students about the move to PBL but some had already experienced difficulties with the approach and there were many myths circulating in the student body that created immediate barriers to teaching and learning. Without a label, PBL has been a straightforward and more successful endeavour for me.

### Lecture less

Less lecturing is an easy lesson but, as I have argued earlier, a hard one to implement in practice. Nevertheless, academia should consider this idea because at their worst, lectures can end up as nothing more than an exercise in passing on huge amounts of basic factual information that adds little to what is already in a textbook or could be summarized in a handout. Less lecturing would happen if lectures were only used for what they do best. If equivalent outcomes can be achieved in some other way, then consider alternatives to the lecture. In this way they would become less frequent, more extraordinary, more valuable and always essential for student experiences and learning. In addition, I find it unacceptable that lecturers are asked to give the same lecture two or three times in a row, or that we use live recordings to relay the lecture to a second (or third) room because student numbers are too large for the main lecture theatre. Let's find another way.

## Summary

In planning for lecturing, start by working out what is really important for students to learn and what might be done better elsewhere. If possible, keep lectures for what they are good at achieving and, for many subjects, a literal interpretation of this suggestion should result in fewer lectures with those remaining attaining a higher quality. Ask yourself what you are adding to the information and knowledge you want students to learn and why providing this in a lecture is necessary.

The realities of teaching in a large institution are not always immediate to new staff but it is important to understand the drivers behind what seems to be required and what is culturally determined and acceptable by peers and students. Understanding does not necessarily mean acceptance, although educational determinations for practice will sometimes have to take second place in decision-making. We may not be as free to teach as we might wish, but being aware of this when it occurs is important.

There are tips for lecturers that can be useful, or even transformational, but as a rule the knowledge each academic brings with them about lecturing is much more valuable. As far as general advice is concerned, it seems reasonable to break the lecture up into smaller structural components and try to engage the student audience. If you do use PowerPoint, do not use it all the time and consider its impact on teaching and learning. Such simplistic advice is, however, complex in the practice context of each unique teaching situation.

I present a guide for lecturers to direct thinking in three important areas for the new academic. I have called this an engagement model and hope it will provide a catalyst for thinking about the art of lecturing:

|  | Illustration of concept |
| --- | --- |
| Performance | There is always an element of live performance in a lecture. The lecturer is centre stage and there are many different types of performance possible. A performer has a deep respect for their audience. Narratives underpin the subject and content. |
| Passion | Loving a subject, being passionate and enthusiastic about an idea and showing genuine care for each student's learning will hold and carry an audience. Learning is a personal and intimate transaction. |
| Purpose | Be clear about the educational rationale for lecturing. What does the teacher want to achieve for students and why? |

*Figure 3.1* Engagement model for lecturing that proposes three concepts for the new lecturer to consider for this mode of teaching

This model essentially endorses the idea that lecturing ought to be practised as an extraordinary experience. Yet it also seems unrealistic to expect routine lecturing to always be exhilarating or captivating, and even if we cut down on the number of lectures we give, some of the audience will still disengage, feel bored or be uninterested. As with all teaching, we can do our best but students are ultimately responsible for their own educational project.

## Thoughts for reflection

1   Some of my colleagues have an aversion to being called a university 'teacher' and insist on the title 'lecturer'. The explanation of the difference between

terms seems to be in the degree that the academic supports and takes responsibility for student learning. In short, teaching is more facilitative of learning whereas lecturing presents opportunities for students, should they wish to avail themselves of these. I have also been informed that teaching is something done in a high school while lecturing differentiates a university education. Although making such distinctions is fraught with difficulty, it seems to say something important about academic identity, how a university lecturer might understand their profession and, importantly, the place of the lecture in this practice and its impact on student learning.

2  Familiarize yourself with the technology in each lecture theatre before teaching and make good use of the technical support each university provides. Being new to an institution provides a good reason for seeking help. Bear in mind that even for those who are familiar with operating the theatre, technology can still fail. This is forgivable. In contrast, those who do not know what they are doing appear incompetent and this is much more difficult to excuse.

3  We often hear of students who are not interested in the lecture and will only learn what is required to pass exams. In contrast we hear little about the lecturer who is not interested in teaching (which might be understandable) or in their subject (which seems incomprehensible). Yet such lecturers do exist and those who appear apathetic and indifferent are probably just as bored as their student audience.

## References

Angelo, T.A. & Cross, K.P. (1993) *Classroom assessment techniques: A handbook for college teachers*, 2nd edn, San Francisco: Jossey-Bass.

Ausubel, D.P. (1968) *Educational psychology: A cognitive view*, New York: Holt, Rinehart and Winston Inc.

Bligh, D. (1998) *What's the use of lectures?* 5th edn, Exeter: Intellect.

Kane, R., Sandretto, S. & Heath, C. (2004) An investigation into excellent tertiary teaching: Emphasising reflective practice, *Higher Education*, 47(3), 283–310.

Mann, S. & Robinson, A. (2009) Boredom in the lecture theatre: An investigation into the contributors, moderators and outcomes of boredom amongst university students, *British Educational Research Journal*, 35(2), 243–58.

Tufte, E.R. (2003) *The cognitive style of PowerPoint*, Connecticut: Graphic Press.

## Further reading

Brown, S. & Race, P. (2002) *Lecturing: A practical guide*, London: Kogan Page.

# Field note 3

## On an imperfect performance

- - - - - - - - - - - - - - - - - - - - - - - - - - - - - -

I volunteered to have a presentation videoed and then sat down after-wards with some of my students to review the recording. It turned out to be one of those significant moments in my development as a teacher. When I watched the tape I was given the remote control and asked by my peer to pause the video at any point that I thought important or would like to discuss with my students.

I stopped the recording after about 55 seconds feeling rather anxious as I relived a dreadful moment at the start of the lecture. The video brought it back with a vengeance. As the introduction got under way, I completely lost my train of thought and had no idea what I was going to say next. My mind had gone blank and there was a long pause, possibly because of the pressure of having a camera focused on me, but also not an unusual event in my teaching.

I explained to the students why I had stopped the video and what I felt at that point. The response surprised me. No one had noticed anything. They could not even see it on the recording.

As we discussed this further they made it clear to me that they don't expect faultless expositions, and 'so what if there is a mistake?' I think I was striving for some sort of perfection in oration, perhaps not under-standing the reality of communicating this way or the degree of tolerance an audience might have.

Since that moment, I have felt much more relaxed about all my presenta-tions and a lot less fearful of lecturing. I believe that if the students know you are trying hard for them, there is an acknowledgement that lecturing can be a messy business.

# Chapter 4

# Discussion as an approach to teaching

## Introduction

Beyond lecturing, a multitude of university teaching methods play out in different ways according to the discipline. These include tutorials, professional skills training, laboratories, workshops, seminars, online discussion and field courses. Sometimes the label we give them is immaterial because lecturers have their own understanding of how they are taught. Yet, when considering such an assortment of methods there is one concept that is relevant to them all, and is a required teaching skill for the vast majority of university lecturers. It concerns teaching and learning through discussion.

Discussion is central to all education and the new lecturer can think about university teaching as a practice divided into: (a) lecturing and (b) everything else, then, in all these other modes of teaching, discussion becomes the primary focus for teaching and student learning. Of course, it is possible to have discussion in a lecture theatre but lecturing is principally about teachers talking and students listening. In contrast, discussion is about participating in discourse where individual performance is usually detrimental and even frowned upon.

Just as students use a variety of approaches to learning, lecturers can *approach* their teaching in different ways. In my argument, discussion becomes an *approach to teaching* rather than a technique applied in class. I ask teachers to imagine planning each class around discussion, with dialogue and inquiry as the primary concern. Consideration would then have to be given to creating conditions for constructive dialogue when selecting any organizational mode. For those teachers working on established courses that already have embedded seminars, laboratories and so on, it is still possible to frame one's teaching approach around discussion.

Discussion, however, also takes place informally and such out-of-class exchanges can be significant to student learning and experiences. For many different reasons the chance corridor conversation can be as valuable as a critical dialogue in a tutorial. Informal discussion has not received much attention in the higher education literature but I will make some brief observations about this part of university life.

Stephen Brookfield and Stephen Preskill (Brookfield & Preskill, 1999) argue that discussion is essentially about a value commitment to teach in a certain way. They would argue that becoming an accomplished discussion teacher not only requires an initial commitment, but continuous attention and practice. Such an approach can be learnt and developed, and to help the novice there are discrete component skills to focus on, plus straightforward ways of organizing classes around discussion. For example, the new teacher can start by developing questioning skills or they can learn how to structure class activities to ensure dialogue takes place. Both strategies will be addressed in this chapter.

The chapter is in four sections. The first considers what we can achieve through discussion and how we might engage students, and the second examines the difficulties students have in discussions and what can be done to overcome this. I then address questioning skills to promote higher-order thinking and conclude with some thoughts on the affective domain – how students feel about discussion and the informal spaces where this is important. Discussion can be a very rewarding experience for both teachers and students and, for critical thinking and skills development, it is vital that it is done well.

## Discussion and student engagement

The objectives for discussion as an approach to university teaching include the following:

1. **To enhance knowledge, understanding and critical thinking**: Cognitive processes are supported through discussion and these are essential to the development of higher-order learning in the discipline. Individuals expand knowledge through discourse in a social situation.
2. **To help students develop values**: Discussion is a central process in value formation. There are certain situations and opportunities that are advantageous for inculcating a range of values that we seek for our students. Circumstances for teaching values include inquiry courses and tutorials.
3. **To induct and educate students into a disciplinary community**: Students have a greater sense of belonging to the discipline because of dialogue. Experience of discussion can change the nature of thinking, feelings and attachment to the subject, department and university.

4. **To educate students in the art of discussion**: Not only can we learn to approach our teaching through discussion, we can also help students in this art; we can teach the subject matter of discussion through tuition, example and practice.

Discussion relies on engagement, talking and listening. A common goal is to develop knowledge and new ways of thinking in a way calculated to help learners come to a better understanding of the subject. In addition, it allows the teacher to find out what each student knows and can do, and this diagnostic opportunity is the foundation of good teaching because it is essential should we wish to treat every learner as an individual (Chapter 5). For students, discussion should help them acquire insight into their own learning processes.

At times, discussion will consist of a simple exchange of views or ideas. However, if we think of discussion taking place in a genuine community of inquiry, then what takes place will also need to challenge the learner. Teachers and students will usually be tested when there are explicit higher-order objectives at stake, for example, discussion for the purpose of enhancing critical thinking. I have yet to meet a lecturer who claims that this sort of activity is easy and it seems that the more demanding our objectives, the less sure we are that we can achieve them. Even when highly structured, discussion can be a messy business with uncertain outcomes.

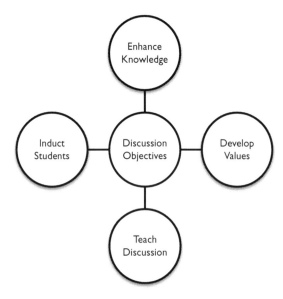

*Figure 4.1* Four objectives for using discussion in university teaching

Elsewhere I have argued that higher education has a responsibility for teaching values even though some academics feel that it is not their responsibility (Harland & Pickering, 2011, p. 43). Learning values and valuing is a consequence of all teaching and this happens either consciously or unconsciously. However, learning values works best when there is explicit recognition of the subject of values within a disciplinary context, and the sorts of spaces that are particularly good for value formation tend to involve discussion in classes such as tutorials or seminars. An example of one such foundational value in the modern university is democracy, and one of the many ways the university can play its part in maintaining liberal democratic principles is through discussion. It has been argued that discussion provides important lessons for a democratic society (Brookfield & Preskill, 1999) and such a value-laden aim requires a specific pedagogy that may include changing traditional roles of authority in teacher–student relationships, designing structures that ensure the possibility each student has a voice, and establishing conditions that allow genuine freedom in participation.

Discussion also adds an important opportunity for socialization in a field of knowledge as students steadily change their disciplinary identities as they negotiate meaning within their chosen community, partly through gaining confidence in the subject and its language. There is also a change in students' emotional connection to their subject and sense of belonging (Wass *et al.*, 2011). They will leave university to take their place elsewhere in the world and ought to feel self-assured in speaking, engaging with others and presenting ideas. Being able to express oneself confidently in university and social and work situations is an essential graduate attribute.

I encourage new teachers to think about their objectives for learning and what qualities and skills they think might be enhanced through discussion. Then, incorporate these specific ideas into written course documents that *explicitly* state that the objective will be achieved through discussion. This strategy clearly signals to both teacher and student the approach to be used in teaching and learning. Students are then directed to think about the learning process and what is expected of them.

## Students don't want to talk

A common objection to discussion is that students, especially in groups, are reluctant to talk, and if they do, they will only respond to direct questions from the lecturer. Such concerns can deter teachers, especially when working with students new to university or when they do not know each other. I can recall many disastrous occasions where my tutorials, seminars or laboratory discussions have fallen flat because I could not get meaningful discussion going. Most colleagues who have attended my professional development workshops on this topic seem to agree; discussion experiences can be brilliant but most of the time getting students engaged requires both careful planning and a high level of teaching skill.

With regards to planning, there are simple strategies that can almost guarantee reasonably balanced discussion. The two tables below describe practical methods for use in tutorials, seminars or workshops. Both work well, even with relatively large numbers of students. If the class is meeting for the first time, make sure personal introductions are made, and for a large class, let this happen after you have put the students into smaller groups.

*Table 4.1* Workshop example (1): Highly structured discussion

| Context: 25 students organized in 5 groups of 5 | |
| --- | --- |
| Stages | Rationale |
| 1 Each student considers an issue and writes a short private response. | If students are new to each other or shy or don't feel safe, then start with an individual exercise. The writing step is important because it provides material to start the discussion. |
| 2 Students share their written responses with others in their group. Discussion starts when all five have contributed. | Talking to a small number of peers about ideas already formulated is supportive as students gain confidence in discussion. When everyone has spoken, the group will feel more comfortable talking and engaging. |
| 3 The workshop is opened up for a more general discussion. | At this point some students feel more confident in their ideas and will be more willing to share them with the larger group. |
| 4 The lecturer collates responses from volunteers or goes round the room systematically. Responses are summarized on the whiteboard. | Ideas are brought together with the lecturer's subject knowledge. The lecturer can use probe or process questioning at this point to explore ideas at a deeper level. Up to this point, the teacher's contribution and voice have been used sparingly. |
| 5 The workshop group are invited to critique the responses summary. | This strategy allows students to rethink their original ideas, critique those from other groups or challenge the lecturer. |
| 6 Each group spends time discussing what has been learnt. | This last task is important in terms of reinforcing learning. It can also be first done at the individual level, and in writing, if necessary. |

*Table 4.2* Workshop example (2): Discussion for a written outcome

*Context: 25 students organized in 5 groups of 5*

| *Stages* | *Rationale* |
|---|---|
| 1 A task is set for students with a fairly tight time limit. Each group is asked to discuss the same task and produce written conclusions on flip-chart paper for others groups to read. | Each student understands that their ideas are to be written out and read by all students and the lecturer. Because of a deliberately tight time frame for the task (e.g. 20 minutes of a 50 minutes class) it is necessary to start talking. Teachers do not interrupt. |
| 2 The charts are hung on the classroom wall. | The written outcomes are public and there is much interest in what other groups have had to say. |
| 3 All students circulate around the classroom to read all the responses. They are primed to look for similarities and differences in reported ideas. | Students critique responses and gather information for the next stage of discussion. |
| 4 The groups sit back down and discuss how their ideas and conclusions compared to others. | The second round of discussion is easier and students know each small group is going to respond to the whole class. |
| 5 The class is opened for general discussion and the teacher ensures that comments are made from each group. All ideas can be explored if relevant. | The teacher has the freedom to take responses from a group spokesperson or from any student. |
| 6 The teacher collates the key outcomes of the exercise on the whiteboard. | Collating the final reviewed list of outcomes brings the exercise together and provides a form of conclusion. |

Such structures, despite being highly controlling, at the very least make sure some discussion takes place; students are engaged and teachers can better manage the balance between teacher and student talk, and between content and process. When there is too much focus on content or seeking a right answer, or when process excludes content, dialogue can be unproductive. Without balance in discussion, the educational experience will be less than ideal because the subject and curriculum will tend to prevail and create a learning experience that leans towards control rather than freedom and initiative. Dewey (1902) recognized this tension in terms of oppositional educational outcomes and such a position can be illustrated in the following continuum that argues for a community-of-inquiry approach that seeks balance in the student learning experience:

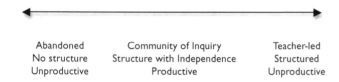

| Abandoned | Community of Inquiry | Teacher-led |
|:---:|:---:|:---:|
| No structure | Structure with Independence | Structured |
| Unproductive | Productive | Unproductive |

*Figure 4.2* A continuum of inquiry and the tension between structure and independence in discussion (adapted from Golding, 2011)

Here the community of inquiry functions under conditions where students can lead discussion but are not left to flounder, and teachers provide enough input to facilitate the process of engagement and ensure that the body of relevant knowledge is not forgotten. However, if critical thinking is an objective, then the teacher ought to consider a further set of skills. If we want students to question an argument or have their ideas subjected to authentic analysis and criticism, then our approach to discussion is likely to require students and teachers to:

- be open-minded;
- feel that their contribution matters;
- be active listeners;
- be willing to engage;
- reconsider arguments;
- carefully examine evidence;
- be tolerant of disagreement;
- trust each other.

In this context, the challenge is not simply to get talk going, but to help students develop an advanced awareness of the purposes of discussion and how they might respond in situations that require critical engagement. This situation requires students to have some insight into their thinking and behaviour.

## Questioning for higher-order learning

In the lecture we can choose whether or not to include discussion. In all other forms of teaching, such as laboratories and tutorials, talk and interaction are expected and so we can shift our teaching approach to prioritize this. Once it becomes central in our thinking, there are many skills that can be identified and mastered. Questioning techniques are one of the most important. Without questioning in discussion, it is difficult to imagine how we might encourage higher-order learning or the evaluative and meta-cognitive skills we wish to see in our students. Not only can the lecturer learn the art of questioning, they can also teach students to ask questions and help them develop this skill.

Asking questions is foundational to evaluative judgement, argument and reasoning and as such they impact on nearly all aspects of learning, including essay writing, listening to a lecture and taking part in a discussion. Questioning provides us with our inner voice so must be at the heart of all inquiry and central to knowledge and values formation. Listed below are three techniques that are easy for beginners to attempt, and when mastered, can be used to enhance learning. These techniques may be considered as a set of technical skills in the first instance; however, when mastered in complex practice situations they will change and take on new meaning. Like other aspects of teaching, the impact of questioning on student learning can be evaluated as part of a teacher's personal inquiry into practice.

*Table 4.3* Techniques for questioning

| Techniques for questioning | Explanation and examples |
| --- | --- |
| Probe questions | These are often secondary questions designed to test an answer or statement or to encourage deeper thinking. Best done when discussion is understood to be exploratory: e.g.<br><br>• Why did you say that?<br>• How does that make you feel?<br>• When might you use such an argument? |
| The right answer | Students enjoy certainty and knowing the right answer. They must also learn that much of the time there is either a best answer or many answers: e.g.<br><br>• Can you think of an alternative?<br>• What else could be happening here?<br>• How well does the evidence support your answer? |
| Wait time | After you receive an answer from a student keep eye contact with them but do not respond straight away. The student will assume you want them to say 'more' and will dig deeper to provide this:<br><br>1 A few seconds' pause is all it takes but students quickly get used to this technique and your expectations.<br>2 After the second response, do not reply but bring others into the discussion and then wait before you say anything. |

## The affective domain

Discussion requires emotional as well as intellectual engagement and both are heightened in the immediacy of face-to-face interactions. Getting to know each student and their learning requires some personal understanding, and this is an important idea if we think of discussion taking place in a community of inquiry. Knowing students allows for very different conversations and a comment made to a stranger can be understood in an entirely different way by someone who is an acquaintance. Similarly, the nature of a critical challenge to someone's contribution depends a lot on how you think that person will take the challenge. Understanding student's personal qualities allows for better judgement and a more nuanced consideration of their values.

Some teaching modes have been transferred to distance or blended learning environments and this reflects the massive interest in the paradigm shift to online discussion (Harasim, 2000). There is a parallel literature consisting of research articles and books that provide evidence on what works, along with good advice on how to get the best out of online teaching. Discussion boards of various types with synchronous and asynchronous designs present many distinct advantages for learning. Research has also shown that there are limitations although to date I am not convinced that the limits are well understood.

Digital space usually provides for collaborations in which students write down their thoughts to engage with each other, and written communication can certainly produce learning of the highest order. However, to think of the digital mobile world of writing as 'discussion', if there is no 'speaking or listening', certainly extends the oral tradition. When I teach online I am essentially communicating in writing, which feels very different from being in the presence of my students and talking to them. There may be engagement of a sort, but human contact provides a distinctive and intimate experience that gives one much more of a sense of connectedness and community. I am reminded that the best university learning experiences reported by the students I interviewed were all related to something that happened when a lecturer was present. Similarly, the residential summer school tutorials that distance educators provide attest to the value of learning in the company of others when possible. There is something about being with other learners that differentiates the more anonymous and less complete experience of text-based digital communication.

There are also certain situations in which discussion occurs more naturally, for example, in student inquiry projects and postgraduate research supervision. There is also unplanned discussion as:

- corridor conversations;
- talking after the lecture;

- students calling in to your office;
- spontaneous activities in class.

Neil Haigh (Haigh, 2005) argues that conversation is something that we can all take for granted but by becoming more self-conscious of it, and with a little thought, we can enhance student learning without destroying the essence of a conversation. When students want to talk after the lecture or when they come to see you out of class, it is normally about clarification and helping them to move on. Students tend to have very specific issues and problems but, if the timing and situation is right, the opportunity can be taken to direct discussion towards other learning possibilities. Such opportunities, sometimes called 'teachable moments', can also occur unexpectedly in class, often when an event allows the teacher to digress from the main topic. These are important because they provide additional opportunities for discussion.

## Thoughts for reflection

1  Students can sometimes be highly competitive and in group situations may not have another's best interests at heart. In many ways, we drive such competitive behaviour by ensuring rewards go to those with the best grades. A student who understands their education in this high-stakes fashion will not jeopardize their marks for the sake of discussion and may decide not to help peers, especially if they see themselves in some form of competitive struggle. Should we then provide marks or grades for 'participation' in discussion?

2  I interviewed a student about the problems they had with discussion. They said 'the adults [lecturers] don't always understand what we have to say' and that 'they can come across as patronizing when they talk down to you'. I asked if this was really discussion and the student reflected for a moment, smiled and said, 'no, it's really being lectured at'.

3  Teachers often provide a high-level of guidance for students to support discussion so why might Brookfield (2006) argue that teacher-guided discussion is an oxymoron?

## References

Brookfield, S.D. (2006) *The skillful teacher: On technique, trust, and responsiveness in the classroom*, 2nd edn, San Francisco: Jossey-Bass.

Brookfield, S.D. & Preskill, S. (1999) *Discussion as a way of teaching: Tools and techniques for university teachers*, Buckingham: Society for Research in Higher Education and Open University Press.

Dewey, J. (1902) The child and the curriculum, Chicago: University of Chicago Press.

Golding, C. (2011) The many faces of constructivist discussion, *Educational Philosophy and Theory*, 43(5), 467–83.

Haigh, N. (2005) Everyday conversation as a context for professional learning and development, *International Journal for Academic Development*, 10(1), 3–16.

Harasim, L. (2000) Shift happens: Online education as a new paradigm for learning, *Internet and Higher Education*, 3, 41–61.

Harland, T. & Pickering, N. (2011) *Values in higher education teaching*, London: Routledge.

Wass, R., Harland, T. & Mercer, A. (2011) Scaffolding critical thinking in the zone of proximal development, *Higher Education Research and Development*, 30(3), 317–28.

## Further reading

Paul, R. & Elder, L. (2006) *The thinker's guide to the art of Socratic questioning*, Dillon Beach, CA: Foundation for Critical Thinking.

# Field note 4
## Working on empathy

- - - - - - - - - - - - - - - -

When I am in the audience of a research seminar, I tend to remain quiet during question time unless I have something to say that I think could make a valuable contribution. What I always worry about is saying something that others might judge as lacking in intelligence. Perhaps I did not hear a key point that others did, or perhaps the rest of the audience understood the argument better than me. I know that when I listen to others respond in the seminar I am highly critical of what they have to say. I guess this is the cut and thrust of an academic life but it can make such experiences simultaneously enjoyable and stressful. Sometimes it takes me a while to process an idea and I always seem to have a 'better' response sometime after the event. I am at my most erudite in private and I have many experiences of: 'I wish I could have said that at the time'.

I think the majority of students probably feel the same when they talk in groups. They too want to appear as if they know what they are talking about and recognize that thinking takes time. If a student does not feel confident in their knowledge and arguments, then they will keep their mouth firmly shut. If I work hard in discussions to make the situation one in which students are encouraged to take a risk and talk, then I also have to face the problem of dealing with factually incorrect responses or poorly argued ideas. Of course, when students are working in groups without me, they also have to negotiate the same problems, but fear of appearing stupid in the company of other students is different again.

Critical discourse usually requires a high level of trust and trust once lost is hard to regain. Sometimes I have to tread carefully as I deal with fragile egos. I have even had students come to me years later to recount a seminar experience that is still painful to them, although I had no idea at the time that there was even an issue. 'I remember when you said ...'

Well, I am afraid I can't remember ...

# Chapter 5

# Theory and practice in student learning

## Introduction

The main reason I have included student learning in an introductory book for new lecturers is that I have witnessed countless teachers undergo a transformation in their thinking as a direct result of being introduced to learning theory. Engaging with ideas around learning can create a liminal moment in a teacher's development with a dramatic shift in focus from thinking about what is taught and the teacher's actions, to what is learnt and what the student does. New lecturers seem to become more considerate about their work and the impact they have on the student experience. In terms of teachers' learning and development, there is a change from reliance on tacit knowledge and experience for guiding practice to recognizing that there are theories out there that have genuine utility. For the novice, focusing on the idea of student learning, as an alternative to the idea of a teacher's teaching, can be a powerful catalyst for change.

The core ideas on learning come mainly from the field of educational and developmental psychology and so we might think of this as a move from small-t theory guiding our actions (for example, knowledge found in case studies or personal knowledge gained from experience), to more classical forms of big-T Theory in which propositions can explain and predict cause and effect in teaching and learning. Higher education has made good use of several psychological and sociocultural concepts to the extent that they are now widely used in teaching courses for university lecturers across the world.

In this chapter, I give a brief introduction to two commonplace theories. The first is called approaches to learning and the second is constructivism. I have selected these because I know they have a good track record for helping university teachers. My aim is to present them as common-sense advice and I support my account with practical examples. Thoughts for reflection come after each theory rather than the end of the chapter.

## Approaches to learning

The basic premise of approaches to learning is that students can set about a learning task with the intent to memorize information (a surface approach) or with the idea that they are going to understand the meaning of the information (a deep approach) (Marton & Säljö, 1976). The teacher's job is to move students from memorizing into a more active mode of learning in which the student seeks to construct conceptual meaning and thus understand the subject at a deeper level. This general theory of learning takes into account how students view knowledge and their understanding of the learning task requirements.

Although approaches to learning may appear as a simple concept, it can have a significant effect on practice because teachers come to understand that whatever they ask students to do causes them to react, in one direction or the other. Because actions are directly connected with learning, teachers can use the theory to make choices about which approach they want in their classrooms. Furthermore, because the idea is dichotomous, the choices the teacher has to make are not great. If we are not promoting deep approaches we get the surface option. Selecting one or the other can also be understood as helping students to learn for better or worse. Importantly, appropriate teaching can change how a student approaches learning and their views of knowledge.

So how can a teacher plan teaching activities with the best chance of getting the approach they want? If you are an advocate for outcomes-led education, then constructive alignment is an idea that may help (Biggs & Tang, 2007). By outcomes education I mean that the intended student learning outcomes are specified during course design, are communicated to students and are assessed and graded after instruction. Not all subjects or learning experiences lend themselves to this strategy and not all academics feel comfortable with outcomes education. However, if the teacher can specify a list of desired outcomes, they can then test to see if these have been achieved and so align teaching and curriculum to ensure that what they ask students to do provides the best possible chance that the outcome requirements will be met. The lecturer needs to create a learning environment and appropriate assessments so that if, for example, they want the learner to 'reflect' or to 'think critically', then they include reflection or critical thinking opportunities in the curriculum, make these explicit and then assess and grade the skill accordingly.

> Where assessment is not aligned to the intended or other desired outcomes, or where the teaching methods do not directly encourage the appropriate learning activities, students can easily 'escape' by

engaging in inappropriate learning activities that become a surface approach to learning. Constructive alignment ... is designed to lock students into deep learning.

(Biggs & Tang, 2007, p. 54)

Constructive alignment also has the potential to create another conceptual shift for the teacher as they now measure their success through what the student has learnt. There tends to be less concern in the curriculum about covering a topic or a subject as more attention is paid to student achievement.

## Thoughts for reflection

In my various academic development roles I have witnessed hundreds of new teachers engage with the approaches to learning with positive outcomes for practice. Many see the concept as a high point of their professional learning, even when they come to understand some of its limitations.

1   My major concern with deep and surface approaches to learning is that the idea is nearly always altered to 'deep and surface learning' (in other words the act of learning rather than the learner's intentions). Because of this, students are labelled as either *deep learners* or *surface learners*. Despite my best efforts, I, too, am guilty of such shoddy use of language, yet this is dangerous because language alters meaning and deep learning has become a proxy for the good learner and surface learning is seen as something bad. Such an interpretation becomes embedded despite the carefully argued theoretical position that deep and surface approaches to learning are mostly responses to the teaching environment while only partially related to personality traits.

2   I am also deeply suspicious of a dichotomous premise that seeks to explain an aspect of human behaviour. It is highly unlikely that deep and surface approaches to learning represent any consistent reality and my own work has shown that the context and the moment can become much more relevant for the choices each student makes towards their learning approach (Kieser *et al.*, 2005). A student recovering from influenza or who is overloaded by course work or hung over after a student party, will probably make different decisions from when they are fit, up to date or have a clear head. Learning is often an unpredictable phenomenon and how a student approaches this on any given day will be complex. Furthermore, the freedom a student has to take an approach

in our mass higher-education systems will always be relative to and often restricted by other demands. Similarly the freedom we have as teachers is limited and we are not always able to organize our teaching in a way we might choose. However, we do know that overall, some things in teaching tend to work better than others, most of the time (given that we know what we want to achieve in the first place).

> I just wish I could learn something without it being for an assessment. I'm also disappointed that I never have time to read around the subject. I think this would be something very interesting to do.
>
> First-year student, second semester

3   If we try to achieve a deep approach to learning through constructive alignment, being specific about learning outcomes can be problematic. Two common objections are that we know students learn many things we value and that we can't measure easily, or at all, and these tend to become marginalized in the minds of both teachers and students in an outcomes-based curriculum. Second, learning can take time and, in modular educational systems, the period allocated may be too short for something to have been truly understood. An outcomes curriculum that sits in a discrete course or semester-long chunk is a very different learning experience for students if we compare this to more extensive learning experiences that take place over two or more years. These longer-term programmes are now rare in universities but still exist in professional subjects like medicine and law.

4   Importantly, the subject dictates outcomes and some subjects are much more open-ended in what they expect of their students, even beyond the types of knowledge typically seen in science, social science, arts and humanities. If outcomes are written in more general terms (e.g. demonstrate critical thinking) then the principles of alignment will still hold the teacher in good stead but they will need a certain amount of tolerance of the unknown because outcomes of this type are difficult to specify with any precision. Those who use learning outcomes as general intentions (objectives), rather than something measurable, may have less of a problem. If a learning outcome can be specified, then this is what the student will usually try to achieve, especially when they are being assessed (see also Chapter 10). Yet we only ever assess a small part of what we would like students to learn and, as part of a longer-term project of developing teaching expertise, the new lecturer should think of all the outcomes they would like to see, not just the easily assessed ones, because this will influence teaching decisions now and in the future and so the type of higher education a student receives.

Despite limitations, a theory of deep and surface approaches can act as a general model and guide to teaching along the lines of: 'What do I have to do to get my students to take a deep approach to their learning?' It pushes students away from memorization and superficial engagement and the lecturer away from didactic teaching. It encourages active modes of learning. However, if the lecturer genuinely wants to teach all students, then deep and surface approaches are not sufficient in themselves because the theory cannot account for the context for learning or the individual learner in a large class.

## Constructivism

The second theory I have chosen is constructivism and it is based on the idea that each learner actively constructs new knowledge by building on their experiences and what they already know. In this theory, constructing meaning defines learning. What the theory asks of the teacher is to recognize the student as an individual learner and find out what they already know and can do before they make decisions about teaching them.

Teachers are frequently thinking about what is happening in class to get some sense of how things are going, but in the constructivist classroom, evaluation takes on a new importance. It becomes more systematic and always focused on the learner's experiences. When planning a curriculum, any decisions about what is taught and why it is taught need to take into account prior student learning. The key task for the teacher is to work less from assumptions and become more informed in their decision-making by finding out about students' knowledge and abilities, and then building on these.

Constructivism describes a wide field of study that includes the socio-cultural theories of Lev Vygostsky (Vygotsky, 1978) and the cognitive psychology of Jerome Bruner (Bruner, 1975). In my teaching I use both ideas to help academics create a practice based on constructivist principles. Vygotsky proposed the zone of proximal development (ZPD) as a model for ascertaining the correct level for starting teaching so that the learner can get the best out of any learning situation. Vygotsky said that the zone of proximal development:

> is the distance between the actual development level as determined by independent problem solving and the level of potential development as determined through problem solving under adult guidance or in collaboration with more capable peers.

(Vygotsky, 1978, p. 86)

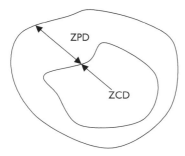

*Figure 5.1* Vygotsky's zone of proximal development. In this model, the zone of current development (ZCD) represents the level that a learner can reach through independent problem solving and the ZPD as the potential distance the learner can reach with the help of a more capable peer (in our case the university teacher). After successful instruction, the outer edge of the ZPD then defines the limits the new ZCD (Harland, 2003)

A lecturer first ascertains the ZCD for whatever they are trying to teach, starts at this point, and then builds on student learning as they steer each student through their ZPD. If the starting point is too far removed from what the student already knows, then they will become lost and if the teacher begins at a point where the subject has already been learnt, then at best the experience provides a recap of prior learning. In large first-year classes, elaborate diagnostic assessments can be done prior to teaching and then the decision about what to teach is made on the basis of the lowest level of knowledge likely to be encountered. There is an understanding of the need to get all students up to speed and on the 'same page'. Sometimes a subject allows for the streaming of students with the intention of bringing them to the same level as others at a later stage; however, streaming on the basis of ability is not a popular strategy in universities in most cases.

So what can a teacher do to help a student pass through the ZPD and reach their full potential? Bruner (1975) is often credited with the term 'scaffolding', which is a metaphor that can guide teachers in their thinking about helping learners travel through the ZPD. Scaffolding is a process in which the learner is given full and appropriate support until they feel confident to apply new skills and strategies independently. When a student is learning a new or difficult task, they are given whatever assistance is necessary. This is the scaffold. As they begin to demonstrate task mastery, the assistance (scaffold) is gradually decreased (dismantled) in order to shift the responsibility for learning from the teacher to the student. Thus, as the student assumes more responsibility for their learning, the teacher provides less support.

The simplest diagnostic tests for informing scaffolding are classroom assessment techniques (Angelo & Cross, 1993). As argued in Chapter 3, CATs' are quick and effective. They not only provide the teacher with information about learners, but they can also be educational for the student. If the lecturer provides good feedback each time a CAT is done, students tend to value the exercise because they see the teacher aligning their teaching with student learning in a considered way.

## Conclusion

In higher education research and development we owe a great debt to educational psychology but I am still not convinced that one particular learning theory is better than another for facilitating a shift in thinking about teaching for the new university lecturer. Whether or not learning theories really have the power to be explanatory, in the sense that they predict cause and effect, is open to debate. Yet the change in practice that comes from engaging with learning theory is often remarkable to see and this on its own makes them worthwhile in any inquiry into university teaching. It would seem that the promise of theory-utility manifests itself in the new lecturer's awareness of a relationship between teaching and learning, and through encouraging new inquiry into the complex nature of practice and its impact on student learning experiences. However, we should not lose sight of the fact that effective teaching and learning may not be related to a greater understanding of theory (because there are brilliant teachers who are ignorant of learning theory).

A final point is that if teaching is largely about telling and that learning is largely about listening and memorizing, then this would equate to an environment where little meaningful activity is taking place if we think of 'meaningful' as something beyond factual information. Any claims to a higher education would be on shaky ground if all we had were telling–memorizing experiences. However, in my experience this caricature of a university education is genuinely rare.

Consider the following:

1   Plan teaching by including simple evaluation strategies so you know what the impact of your teaching (and any changes you have made) has had on student learning.
2   Document your thoughts on student learning and the data from evaluations; file this away and read it before you next teach the course.
3   Be flexible and introduce (small) changes to suit the majority of learners.
4   Have strategies for picking up those who fall either side of the majority.

5   Make sure you are clear about what you want to achieve because what you ask students to do often determines what you get. Engaging with a critique of a conceptual idea is very different from memorizing factual knowledge. Both can be important but it is still the teacher who decides on the type of curricular experiences their students receive.

6   Remember that assessed components of a curriculum are the main drivers for student effort and therefore have a major impact on learning.

Application of theory is seldom straightforward in the complex world of practice where constraints often make our aspirations difficult or even impossible. In addition, we need to understand the theory–practice gap that is caused partly by how our understanding of theory shifts as practice changes. Schön (1987) would argue that 'theory-in-use' and theoretical knowledge require careful integration.

## Thoughts for reflection

1   In certain subjects, for example mathematics, the teacher can gain high-quality insight into each of their student's capabilities. Yet other subjects, for example history or zoology, are likely to pose more of a challenge.

2   If the environment is too structured and controlled, then the learner has no room to build on their knowledge and experiences so we need constructivist curricular experiences that encourage exploration and discovery. These typically include research training, inquiry tasks and problem-based learning (PBL).

3   Apparently today's students want to be spoon-fed and if this is true, then how do we motivate them to take more responsibility in the constructivist classroom? This problem needs careful consideration, especially if students are moving between different teachers and between a more traditional and a constructivist course.

4   When teaching takes into account constructivism, the teacher's identity alters and a common way of explaining this shift is to say that we are no longer teachers but facilitators of learning. However, what then happens is the facilitator is seen as 'good' and the (traditional) teacher as 'bad' and when you set such rhetoric against the political climate of teacher-subjugation and how teaching as a profession is generally seen by society (anyone can teach), the title facilitator can be seen as either offensive or an irritating politically correct term. I like to defend the values of teaching and will always be proud to call myself a teacher.

5   In this account, I am using learning and development interchangeably as we are dealing with adults. However, Vygotsky (1978) argued that

learning leads the developmental stage and that the stage can be in advance of what is expected. This idea is important when thinking about learning because one of the most common arguments I hear is that students can't do something because they are first years, or they have no experience or lack the right background, and so on. In my teaching, I work hard to push students way beyond what is typically expected and have found that many turn out to be far more capable than I have given them credit for.

## References

Angelo, T.A. & Cross, K.P. (1993) *Classroom assessment techniques: A handbook for college teachers*, 2nd edn, San Francisco: Jossey-Bass.

Biggs, J. & Tang, C. (2007) *Teaching for quality learning at university*, Maidenhead: McGraw Hill and Open University Press.

Bruner, J. (1975) From communication to language. A psychological perspective, *Cognition*, 3, 255–89.

Harland, T. (2003) Vygotsky's zone of proximal development and problem-based learning: Linking a theoretical concept with practice through Action Research, *Teaching in Higher Education*, 8(2), 263–72.

Kieser, J., Herbison, P. & Harland, T. (2005) The influence of context on student's approaches to learning: A case study, *European Journal of Dental Education*, 9(4), 150–6.

Marton, F. & Säljö, R. (1976) On qualitative differences in learning: I. Outcome and process, *British Journal of Educational Psychology*, 46(1), 4–11.

Schön, D. (1987) *Educating the reflective practitioner*, London: Jossey-Bass.

Vygotsky, L.S. (1978) *Mind in society: The development of higher mental processes*, Cambridge, MA: Harvard University Press.

## Further reading

Ramsden, P. (1992) *Learning to teach in higher education*, London: Routledge.

# Field note 5
## Mobile phones
- - - - - - - - - -

I was asked recently to peer review a colleague in the medical school giving a lecture. At the start I was surprised to see students handing in their mobile phones and putting them in a pile on a desk in front of the lectern. All through the lecture, I could not help feeling that it was a little draconian but at the same time I was unexpectedly impressed. I thought that if a lecturer can get away with this strategy, well, it stops a suite of possible misbehaving: phones going off, texting, tweeting, accessing the Internet and playing games.

I had to raise this in our debriefing session and felt such a fool when I was told that they were not mobiles but digital tape recorders mostly belonging to students whose first language was not English. In the high-stakes competitive world of the health sciences, it seemed to me that these students were leaving nothing to chance.

# Chapter 6

# Students past and present

## Introduction

In this chapter I would like to explore two contemporary debates concerning students. The first is the changing nature of the relationship between students and the university in the move to mass higher education. In this argument, students live under the shadow of neoliberal political reform where economics has become more central to everyone's lives and the world is experienced and offered principally as a place for the individual to accumulate capital in a competitive free-market. The second issue is that technology has created a 'new generation' of students who are somewhat different from those of the past, and thus many of our own experiences as teachers. I conclude the chapter with some thoughts on what we might reasonably expect from a university student.

## Students as customers

Since the radical economic and political reforms of the late 1970s and early 1980s, higher education has started on a journey of transformation as it deals with the impact of neoliberal ideology. Neoliberal thinking is founded on a belief that the market and free competition are superior to state intervention for bringing about societal change. The state withdraws from economic and social activities and adopts a new role in legislation to ensure competitive markets function and personal freedom is maximized.

When such ideological reform came to the public institutions, including the state-owned university sector, change was difficult (Kelsey, 1998). The positive conception of freedom in which the state actively intervenes to shape the individual as a competitive entrepreneur does not sit easily within the public university and full privatization of state-owned universities has not been possible. However, new systems of funding, governance and mechanisms to control the core activities of research and teaching have resulted in universities becoming more entrepreneurial and less reliant on government and taxpayer support.

The recent changes that led to mass higher education have been part of the reform agenda and are likely to have been driven for economic reasons (knowledge as a valuable commodity and concurrent economies of scale in teaching), rather than to create a more just society in which all those who can benefit from a higher education gain access. Higher education is seen through the lens of 'enterprise' because of its role in producing both knowledge and students for the new knowledge industries (Harland, 2009). Academics are now cast as human capital in a global market place (Harland *et al.*, 2010).

The student body has grown dramatically since the late 1970s and there has been diversification in both social and educational backgrounds, despite wealthier families benefiting disproportionately from greater access to higher education. The elite quality of university education now manifests itself not from the student body but through careful selection of students and differentiation of universities that are ranked and viewed by society as 'good' or 'second rate' and so on. It is not difficult to compile a shortlist of the world's top universities or the most desirable ones to attend in any country.

Such ideas about change in the operation and culture of our universities may not seem to have immediate relevance to the new lecturer but this is not the case because they need to practise in the context of reductions in state subsidy, gradual increases in student 'consumer' charges and the need to teach a diverse student body. Even in higher education systems where there is a history of student financial contribution, such as the USA, the amount paid is increasing dramatically. In Western public education systems, the state is not prepared to fully subsidize university students and the student is picking up a much larger share of the cost of their education.

A student who pays high fees and borrows money for subsistence is likely to think very differently about teaching and learning than a student who has their fees and maintenance paid through a private or taxpayer-funded scholarship. New university lecturers (many of whom will also be paying off student loans) will need to consider their relationship to students in an appropriate way. Are we there to provide an opportunity for all students to study and learn or are we there to 'deliver' an education through our lectures and tutorials? The idea of reading for a degree has largely disappeared except in the elite institutions, and students and teachers expect something more tangible to be provided as a product to support learning. Students are empowered to demand we provide a decent education as a return on their investment. The language of higher education is now replete with such industrial metaphors.

One of the university's most important tasks is maintaining standards and the value of qualifications and this is under threat as institutions come under pressure to ensure failure rates across the student body are low. In any democratic higher education system, students should have the freedom to learn and the freedom to fail, but teacher and university accountability and compliance make either outcome more difficult. The neoliberal universities compete with each other for status, students and funding, while their authority is increasingly undermined.

These ideas will play out very differently across disciplines and students have migrated from humanities to sciences and from sciences to applied subjects. Students want good jobs after such a large financial investment and so are prepared to see themselves as human capital from an early stage at university.

## A Net generation of students

It has been claimed that contemporary students, particularly in Western educational systems, are different from those of the past. They have grown up entirely in a world of advanced technology as 'digital natives' and are said to belong to the 'Net generation' because their lives have been influenced substantially by the revolution in computing and information technologies of the last three decades.

The demands that are frequently heard are that we have to redesign our educational systems to meet students' new learning preferences and needs. Yet there is little evidence that our digital natives are so different from students of the past and there is much more evidence that our educational systems keep pace with change, or are sometimes even ahead. Just look at your own university library (or whatever name it goes by now) and it will bear only a slight resemblance to the libraries of a few decades ago. One could use other examples such as our course management systems, the use of PowerPoint as a digital presentation medium and the technology available in lecture theatres. Universities do change and academics and students embrace new technologies, largely with great enthusiasm.

Common sense dictates that it is unlikely that students have undergone rapid evolution into some new type of hominid. Yet even if the assertion that they somehow have new ways of learning is correct, should we teach to whatever their new preferences and styles might be? My answer would be simple – no. As part of their education, students need a wide range of learning experiences and many of these will be unique to a university and form the very fabric of higher learning. Such an array will include the use of technology where appropriate. Furthermore, in a mass higher-education system, students are unlikely to have the same preferences and so meeting any stated needs for all is nigh on impossible (most of the time).

I am sure that students do have preferred learning styles, especially if these equate to strategies that have proved successful for them in the past. In addition, there is good evidence that they will change their approaches to learning depending on the task required of them (see Chapter 5). However, the revolutionary appeals for the ending of university education as we know it seem a little premature. The claims made by those proposing radical change, on the basis that university education was not designed for the people we now teach, suggest that students today are active experiential learners, are good at multi-tasking and dependent on computers for information and communication (Bennett *et al.*, 2008). I would counter that students can be all of these things but we simply have no evidence that they are fundamentally changed as learners and so making any reasonable judgement about wholesale revision of teaching is premature; just because students seem to spend a great deal of time on the Internet or mobile phone does not mean that our education system is inadequate.

Lest you think that I am a neo-Luddite, I am a lecturer who has experienced the world before and after the computing revolution. I have witnessed the arrival of pocket calculators, the personal computer, the Internet and email. I have embraced them all and they have changed my life and the way I work, and I would not wish to function in alternative ways. Like many of my fellow academics, I may wish I did not get so many emails and I often feel swept along by the technology-driven pace at which academic life now flows. I wish, for example, I had more time to read and think. But the advantages of technology always seem to outweigh the disadvantages in this equation and it is hard for me to imagine a world without the Internet, computers and other forms of digital technology. Allow me to repeat: the medium is the message.

My students do not seem much different either. They may text on their mobile phones underneath their desks during a lecture rather than carve their names in the desk. They may prefer PowerPoint handouts to note taking. They may watch less television and spend more time on a computer. But these differences seem marginal. What is important is that I can plan for curriculum experiences that include good digital communication, that I can assume nearly all my students will have a laptop or easy access to a computer, that I can now expect a higher quality of evidence in the work I set, and that I have a few new tasks to attend to, such as looking out for cut-and-paste plagiarism.

If you decide to read more about the digital native debate you will find that many of the issues raised appear very theoretical, rather than practical. Because of this I decided to re-examine a common task that I have given to university students over the last 25 years to see how this might have changed. The task is a science project on a topic that requires authentic practical work and a literature review:

*Table 6.1* Student approaches to a science research project past and present

| Student requirements | Today | 25 years ago |
|---|---|---|
| Become familiar with the literature. | Easy access to the Internet and electronic journals. Some books only in the library. Store articles as PDFs on computer. Use bibliographic management software. | Search and browse journals and books on the library shelves, photocopy relevant articles or make notes. Arrange for inter-loans or send postcards to request article reprints. |
| Formulate a hypothesis and question. | As 25 years ago. | |
| Design an experiment. | As 25 years ago. | |
| Carry out the experiment. | As 25 years ago. | |
| Analyse the data. | Store, organize and manipulate data with a spreadsheet program. Use statistics packages and graphics software. | Data written out on paper. Calculators and hand-drawn graphs. |
| Interpret the results. | As 25 years ago. | |
| Write a report. | Word processing, easy cut and paste, spelling and grammar check. | Handwritten. |
| Redraft report. | Internet search provides additional evidence, easy partial redrafting. | Return to the library for new evidence. Often a full new draft. |

In the table, it can be seen that the library now comes to the student and that the ease of accessing and processing information radically changes the nature of what can be achieved. However, if the student of 25 years ago made do with the relatively limited information they were likely to access on a library visit, does this mean that students of today will retrieve more just because searching is so much easier and quicker? The new ways of working are certainly faster but has it produced better learners or higher quality thinking? Reading a scientific paper still requires a critical mind and good evaluative judgement focused on the quality of evidence and argument.

Project data can also be handled and analysed with great efficiency using computers but we have also sacrificed the theoretical knowledge behind the statistical procedures and, even more importantly for my science discipline, knowledge about the proper application of statistical methods. Typically I find students going through the analysis in a poorly conceived manner, often using fancy statistical proofs that are possible, not required and usually not understood.

The major difference seems to come in writing reports. Writing using a word processing package is far removed from writing with pen and paper. The speed at which changes can be made or more data and ideas brought in is remarkable. However, I am not convinced that this fast information-processing–thinking flow and easy production necessarily improves learning or the quality of the final product. I think it does change the teacher's expectations of what can be achieved in a set time and it changes our tolerance to technical errors (e.g. there is no longer any excuse for incorrect spelling or poor grammar).

In the example given in Table 6.1 I recognize that the steps in such a science project are neither precise nor discrete. However, certain aspects have remained the same for the last 25 years and these tend to sit in the critical domain of knowledge and learning, and are the stages that require careful thought and creativity that is not necessarily tied to technological advance. Most of the digital revolution seems to provide faster and greater access to information for many people across the world but in the context of a university education, this change also impacts on both learning and how we understand and value knowledge. Yet whatever the assumed benefits and costs, there does not seem to be enough evidence that the digital revolution requires us to respond with wholesale changes to higher education.

## What might we reasonably expect of our students?

We might expect students to master a received body of knowledge that consists of the established facts and theories of the discipline. This requirement is particularly important in the sciences where empirical forms of knowledge are learnt in a stepwise manner. In humanities-type subjects, more emphasis is placed on analysis and interpretation and students are usually required to form their own views. However, what all university students should be able to do is stand back from their learning and make decisions about knowledge, have insight into themselves as learners and develop their own values. Learning to be creative and imaginative critical thinkers (Chapter 10) and learning about oneself are both part of student identity formation. University experiences become a schooling of the mind and this is why the academic subject expert also needs to be a teaching expert (Chapter 1).

## Thoughts for reflection

1  If students graduate from our university and then act largely as individuals in a competitive free market, where economic imperatives outweigh broader societal concerns, have we fulfilled our role as educators for society? However important we consider the economy and jobs, these are still only one aspect of the university mission and only partly reflect what it means to have an education that is higher in some way.

2  When students arrive at university, they have little idea of what to expect. We could teach them entirely in lecture classes of 500 or only in tutorials. We can train them as researchers from day one or spend three years preparing them to start research at a postgraduate level. We still have a lot of freedom. The new academics I work with repeatedly tell me that they are constrained because new entrants are not capable of undertaking certain activities, usually for the reason that high school has not prepared them adequately. My own experiments with curriculum suggest that academics are mostly wrong in this assertion and seriously underestimate the capacity of their new students.

3  According to Furedi (2004) we no longer show students respect by assuming that they need assistance in anything they find difficult. Furedi calls them 'fragile children' and this concept informs the thinking behind the formation of student-learning support centres in many universities. These are generally central university service units that ensure students across the disciplines get assistance and support in areas such as study skills, essay writing and exam techniques. The rationale behind student support is that a higher education is too demanding for many, and that it is the university's responsibility to do something about this. Furedi would argue that ultimately the extra support we provide re-enforces a low expectation of students and a dumbing down of standards and intellectual life.

## References

Bennett, S., Maton, K. & Kervin, L. (2008) The 'digital natives' debate: A critical review of the evidence, *British Journal of Educational Technology*, 39(5), 775–86.

Furedi, F. (2004) *Where have all the intellectuals gone? Confronting 21st Century philistinism*, London: Continuum.

Harland, T. (2009) The university, neoliberal reform and the liberal educational ideal. In M. Tight, J. Huisman, Ka Ho Mok & C.C. Morphew (eds), *The Routledge international handbook of higher education*, London: Routledge.

Harland, T., Tidswell, T. Everett, D., Hale, L., & Pickering, N. (2010) Neoliberalism and the academic as critic and conscience of society, *Teaching in Higher Education*, 15(1), 85–96.

Kelsey, J. (1998) Privatizing the universities, *Journal of Law and Society*, 25(1), 51–70.

## Further reading

Freire, P. (1970) *Pedagogy of the oppressed*, New York: Seabury Press.

Marginson, S. & Considine, M. (2000) *The enterprise university. Power, governance and reinvention in Australia*, Cambridge: Cambridge University Press.

# Field note 6
## On anonymity

When I interviewed the students for this study, the most striking aspect of their stories of university life was how anonymous they could be within the system. Surrounded by thousands of people but feeling, at times, quite alone. One student had not spoken to anyone in the first two years and then one day knocked on her lecturer's office door. She left that room a different person after a brief and friendly exchange that helped her to finally understand a difficult theory. But she also left with offers of further help and a feeling of overwhelming kindness. Something so simple and routine for the lecturer altered her perceptions of university life, boosted her confidence and changed her as a learner. Although such a story might appear extreme, all 24 of those interviewed commented on how important it had been to get to know their teachers. Yet, in the early stages, students simply 'did not talk to the lecturers'. So when does communication start?

There was also evidence that learning higher-order skills in the discipline required a good relationship between teacher and student and if we want to understand students as learners, we need to understand them as people. Yet many of my students are anonymous to me and I can blame large classes, modular teaching and the pressures and pace of academic work. But only partially.

I was considering these issues the other day in class and decided to ask a few of my second years how things were going and which subjects they were enjoying most. Then I asked them to explain their choices – was it the topic or something else? The answers were complex but how their lecturers taught and how they treated students, were crucial in every response. Students disliked one department where they felt like they were treated as schoolchildren. They did not think that university should be like this.

I came away thinking how much I learnt from taking a few minutes to inquire into students. Perhaps I should seek out those lecturers the students liked and try and find out how they organized and taught their courses. What did they do, what were their values? I also wondered why the students were so forthcoming and would talk to me so openly about my fellow lecturers.

# Chapter 7

# Research and the new academic

## Introduction

In general it is true to say that research is prized above all other activities in a university, and within the research-intensive sector, in particular, it is the currency for a profitable career. Rightly or wrongly, in this context the task of teaching comes second, although teaching is always espoused as a fundamental value and, for many, it is their principal reason for coming to work each day. It is difficult to see these circumstances changing in the future despite much effort directed at raising the relative status of teaching. Small successes in this quest have been made from time to time and an example from the UK is the academic who is promoted to an ad hominem chair on the basis of the quality of their teaching and contribution to scholarship: it now appears possible, but it is still very rare and perhaps tokenistic.

The activities of research and teaching often feel quite separate with respect to how each task is structured and the way academic life is organized. Putting research and teaching into distinct compartments is a logical way of dealing with these aspects of work. University teaching is intended to be research-led and the creation and dissemination of knowledge exemplify the idea of the university. The university teacher is expected to be a researcher and ideally the researcher of the subject being taught. When both activities are present in the same person, there is particular benefit to the student and, it is argued, a reciprocal benefit for research and teaching. In this chapter I report what new academics say about their disciplinary research and provide some alternative ways of thinking about this activity and its relationship with teaching.

## What new academics say about research

There are three recurring themes that emerged from concerns expressed in mentoring groups. These are:

1   Research is put on hold while academics deal with the immediate demands of writing lectures, teaching and settling into a new workplace.
2   New academics feel continuous pressure from not doing research but are more optimistic when they have identified a future period in which they will catch up.
3   New academics experience the tension caused by research and teaching competing with each other but have not thought a lot about how these activities are linked, beyond the fact that they teach in their research area.

### Putting research on hold

Being overwhelmed by teaching at the start of a new academic job is understandable and there is nothing that focuses the mind of a novice like delivering a set of new lectures to a large number of students or conducting a series of worthwhile tutorials. Although the immediacy of teaching demands is usually a reality for new staff, it is also true for many novices that lecturing can be a terrifying experience. I have even come across lecturers late in their career who have never got past feeling acute anxiety before entering a lecture theatre.

At the same time, it is not a good idea to leave research until the next break or the end of the term because it is easy to lose momentum and at the same time be drawn into other academic tasks that seem to fill up each working day. When this happens, it quickly becomes very difficult to free oneself of jobs. The new academic requires the space to do both research and teaching from day one and if this becomes a problem the solution needs to come from the academic, their colleagues and head of department.

### Catching up

Of course, it is possible to catch up on research at a later date, but the catching-up period is always longer than predicted. If it is put off until the next break, the academic finds that the break is not always as empty as might have been forecast and also that they genuinely need a period of rest and recuperation. The evidence I have from those who have chosen this strategy is that research slowly recovers but the period lost is substantially more than expected. It is also harder to catch up on other aspects of research, for example, planning for the next generation of researchers through attracting postgraduates, developing research conversations in wider communities and contributing to the research environment. For the relatively inexperienced researcher who has just completed a PhD, their focus should be on writing for publication. Getting out of the habit of regular writing can be one of the most difficult to re-establish. Writing skills are generally hard won, take time to master and need regular attention.

*Research and teaching*

The relationship between the two activities only seems important to new academics when there is stress caused by having to do one or the other. It is seen as a workload and career issue. In general, I have found that when academics are teaching, this takes time away from research (this proposition is never expressed the other way round). With my mentoring groups, I encourage a much fuller debate on the relationship between research and teaching (see 'The relationship between research and teaching' below) because this issue is fundamental to understanding academic practice and developing a reasonably fulfilling academic career. In saying this, I think it is still realistic for a university academic to have the opportunity to teach and research to the best of their ability without feeling one activity gets in the way of the other.

*What can be done?*

For early career staff, there are some common practical strategies that require combined action from the individual, department and academic community. These can include:

- a half-time teaching load in the first year (with colleagues sharing the extra work this creates);
- blocking off research time each week;
- resisting taking on administrative and committee work;
- being invited to join an established research group;
- mentoring support and regular checks to make sure that things are going well and the academic feels supported.

Too often, I see new academics who are expected to be both independent and successful from day one. For some reason, they often have the same expectations of themselves.

## The relationship between research and teaching

There is a long-standing and rather prolific debate about how research is understood in our universities (e.g. Barnett, 1990) and in particular its relationship with teaching (e.g. Brew & Boud, 1995). I have thought carefully about the complex nature of the association and have shifted my ideas many times. My present position is that research is the foundation of university teaching and I agree with the NZ position that a defining characteristic of a university is that teaching is done by researchers (Education

Act, 1989). I feel that if a university does not see research as the core function for its teaching staff, the institution should take on a different name. In countries where there is no unified university sector, such as the USA, such an idea is likely to be seen as contentious or divisive, although institutions that do not see themselves as research-intensive need to ask themselves where the knowledge they use comes from, and what they gain or lose by focusing on teaching and teachers who are not research active. In addition, I argue that teachers should be researchers of the subject their own practice (Chapter 1).

In the research-intensive universities, the experiences of research and teaching as discrete activities comes partly from the fragmentation of academic life and competing pressure from each of the many functions academics are now expected to perform and be accountable for. Each task is appreciated differently depending on the context in which it is valued. A cliché that illustrates how work activities are valued is the common assertion that anyone can teach but only the best minds can do research. Research is often carried out independently of teaching (say in a research institution) and it is usually so specialized that a direct link between the subject being researched and a subject taught can be tenuous, especially at an undergraduate level.

To provide a different way of thinking about academic work, I encourage all new academics to think about teaching and research as one and the same activity. I use either a 'purposes' argument or a 'methods' argument to make this point, but both reconceptualize research-as-teaching or teaching-as-research:

### (a) Research and teaching share the same purposes

Research is a specialized form of teaching. I suggest this because the outcome of research is that someone learns something. If no one learnt anything, then the research would be a waste of time. Similarly the purpose of teaching is to help someone learn something. Teaching that does not lead to learning is also a waste of time. In research, we tend to teach our peers and colleagues first (through published papers, conferences and research seminars), and then our students. Nevertheless, the primary purpose of research is teaching for learning.

### (b) Research is a method of learning and teaching

Research is done in many places: in the home, industry, government and private research institutes and, of course, in universities. But universities are fairly unique because they teach and award degrees. Not all institutions of higher education see research as a core activity but I would argue that research is foundational to the university:

1   If an academic undertakes research and publishes original ideas, then they have to become an expert in their subject with expertise that goes beyond discovering something and then teaching it. To put your ideas in the public domain and respectfully make use of established knowledge and theories requires a deep understanding of a subject and discipline.

2   University teachers should contribute to their field as well as taking and using research knowledge from others.

3   A primary purpose of research is to help oneself and others learn about new findings. Another is to use the knowledge already out there to help others learn.

4   If we want students to learn to be inquirers or researchers or use methods of inquiry and research in their education, then the teacher needs that experience too. It is essential they are experts in research processes to guide students adequately. This expertise includes an important subset of attributes such as being able to critique ideas and make evaluative judgement.

5   'Straight from the horse's mouth', where nothing is 'lost in translation', are two idioms that illustrate why learning with the person that created the knowledge in the first place is usually a good idea. Yet researchers often teach more broadly in their field and outside their research area. This matters less than one might think because the research mind is applied to other knowledge areas and a researcher brings these attributes to the teaching and learning transaction.

6   As I argued in Chapter 1, academics can also teach 'themselves' to be teachers. A good researcher applies their research skills to their own professional learning. This concept should be both culturally acceptable and emancipatory in the sense that it gives academics the freedom to pursue their own learning and development agenda. Whether or not this is seen as measurable research (in terms of, say, a published research paper) or non-measurable research (discovering knowledge that changes teaching), it is still a method of learning and teaching.

Such arguments may also help in making a case for research as the foundation of all aspects of academic work. In this sense, I also like to think of actively directing research skills towards professional development as part of an academic apprenticeship. This idea, because it is not necessarily intuitive, requires a rethink of academic life and then a commitment to self-determination and a critical mind directed towards an inquiry into one's own work and life. Like all research, it will be done with the help of others of a similar disposition and those experienced enough to help.

## Thoughts for reflection

1  In Robert Boice's ten-year study of new academics (Boice, 1992) he concludes that writing is one the most difficult skills for academics to master. The conclusions of this study still resonate with those I work with and any support for writing is always well received by academics. Writing is a hard part of any research study and because of this, success for some academics remains elusive. Boice's main recommendations are to develop the habit early, write frequently, share early drafts and accept criticism.

2  Ideas about research and teaching links differ and it is important to distinguish between how academics, their departments or their course teams see this link. Thoughts on research and teaching will be partly related to personal academic identity but also strongly influenced by departmental work culture. For the new academic, certain values that do not sit easily within the cultural frameworks in which they work may have to be put on hold.

3  Lewis Elton proposes that the link between research and teaching is dialectic and is best when teaching is student-centred, something akin to a joint inquiry between student and teacher (Elton, 2001). So 'the nature of the link between research and teaching depends primarily on the process of the student curriculum, rather than the outcomes of either research or teaching' (p. 49). One fact is sure: without research there can be no university teaching and without teaching, there is no point in doing research.

## References

Barnett, R. (1990) *The idea of higher education*, Buckingham: Society for Research in Higher Education and Open University Press.

Boice, R. (1992) *The new faculty member*, San Francisco: Jossey-Bass Inc.

Brew, A. & Boud, D. (1995) Teaching and research: Establishing the vital link with learning, *Higher Education*, 29, 261–73.

Education Act (1989) *Part 14 Establishment and disestablishment of tertiary institutions*, S162, 4(a)(v), New Zealand Government.

Elton, L. (2001) Research and teaching: Conditions for a positive link (1), *Teaching in Higher Education*, 6(1), 43–56.

## Further reading

Brew, A. (2006) *Research and teaching: Beyond the divide*, London: Palgrave Macmillan.

# Field note 7
## Telling your story

On the whole, no one will ask you to talk about or explain your work, not even your department colleagues. If you want to be heard, then you must work out a way of telling your own research story and in such a way that others will listen. Narrative competence is a measure of a successful researcher and something I did not recognize until later in my career.

You will be invited to give a department seminar, put yourself forward for conference presentations and send your work to journals. These are typical situations in which you can publish ideas, but in themselves they are not sufficient. I am convinced that those who use every opportunity to tell a compelling story have the most success.

This argument is reflected in Thomas Khun's thoughts on scientific revolutions and the observation that some ideas gain traction while others fall by the wayside because of social, cultural and historical circumstances, rather than just scientific merit (Khun, 1962).

As I embarked on my own journey as a higher education researcher, I decided to trace ideas back in history to their origins and was initially surprised by how so much in my field has been said before, is repeated or rediscovered. Why did a later author gain so much in reputation from an idea when the older historical accounts were ignored? Why do only a few researchers appear to monopolize the field?

Think of yourself as the narrator of your own research story.


Khun, T. S. (1962) The structure of scientific revolutions, Chicago: University of Chicago Press.

# Chapter 8

# Academic work

## Introduction

In 2002 Ann Austin raised the possibility that in the near future academic work would be differentiated to such a degree that we no longer had the all-round academic, but experts who specialized in particular areas of academic work (Austin, 2002). Despite the appeal that such an idea might still hold for those who control and manage our universities, and the evidence of increasing diversity in academic roles, the archetypal lecturer post is still the norm and seems likely to remain so for a long time. Because of this situation, the chapter focuses on the concerns of lecturers taking up their first position with responsibilities for teaching, research, service and administration. Most of my academic development work is with this staff group and during the last 15 years or so there are two related issues on which I have been regularly asked for advice. These are how to manage time and what a reasonable and fair teaching load might be.

That these requests have been repeated year in, year out, have prompted me to look for what lies behind them and, as I explore these in this chapter, I will also examine the department as a site of induction for the new academics. Induction is pivotal to balance in academic work. It is partly about getting the right information in a timely fashion, but new academics also need to feel supported in their work and valued by colleagues. Poor guidance at this early stage can have huge implications for future careers.

## Time management

New academics want to know how to manage their time. This constantly recurring issue is obviously important to this group but it is also very difficult to give advice, especially suggestions that make a real difference. Unfortunately neither self-help books nor the wisdom of experienced academics seem to have much genuine utility for the new academic and managing time is something that has to be worked on constantly by the individual over the first few years of practice.

The moment an academic is in post, they typically feel overwhelmed, overworked and stretched thinly. The idea of a structured working week with clear boundaries fast becomes an illusion. These feelings seem to be caused by a number of complex factors including the freedom each academic has to structure work, the fact that research has no limits, having to deal with large numbers of students and a panopticon university culture that manages to create the impression that it is normal for everyone to work long hours.

Furthermore, each academic seems to bring distinctive skills and talents to higher education. Job requirements are based on unique fields and specialties and only loosely framed around the core of teaching and research. On top of this, academics are reasonably free to make many work decisions while, at different times, face strict requirements to perform certain activities. Furthermore they report that a large portion of work is hard to define or account for. It is this mixture of different roles, and freedom and constraint in an indeterminate working week that results in good time management practice being difficult to implement. Yet the new academics I work with still seek technical solutions to the problem of managing their activities.

One common tool is workload planning and workload models now seem to be commonplace. I have examined a variety of models that specify tasks and the time to be spent on them and I would conclude that overall they do not serve their purposes well. They may even have a detrimental impact on individuals and department culture. These impacts seem to be independent of the model's intricacy and the greater the complexity, the more time it takes to administer them.

I am yet to be convinced that a workload model designed for a group of academics or a department has helped anyone in a university manage their time, although those who have invested energy in such initiatives often defend them. Arguments in their favour are not very persuasive and I genuinely doubt they have much of a positive impact on working life. Of course a model allows a group of academics to feel as though they are being just and transparent so that no one gets an unfair advantage (usually through carving out more research time than someone else). Models also allow departments to feel they are managing work in a responsible manner even though the idea that academic work can be 'managed' in some way remains a moot point.

One of the more complex systems I looked at took into account different tasks and skill sets and weighted each one in terms of how long it takes to complete an activity (for example, an academic is allocated so many points for a successful grant, so many for each postgraduate student, so much per teaching hour and so on). These activities, within limits, were then traded against others. So an academic with a high postgraduate supervision load might teach fewer undergraduate courses, or a research team with a large grant might buy out teaching altogether. Yet even this model only described how work might be allocated while doing nothing to help with an individual's time management. In fact, it created considerable 'extra' administrative work for everyone in the department, including form filling, justification and negotiation in meetings. I wondered if it just described what the academics would have done anyway, and whether or not it had been introduced strategically to replace collegial discussion with policy.

I propose that for the new academic, nothing improves much on the simple 2/2/1 model characteristic of the older research-intensive universities: two days spent on research, two days for teaching and one day for administration, service and everything else. This version seems to have evolved quite naturally over many decades as a reasonable expectation of academic work and reflects both an ethical partitioning and holistic view of work activity. However, given the cyclical nature of academic work and the rather elastic working week (on average 50 hours; Staniforth & Harland, 1999), a 2/2/1 five-day model seems rather optimistic. It does, however, provide a simple and useful guide to balancing core activities for those working in research-intensive universities.

What is probably most effective in time management is for the new academic's head of department to be explicit about what they, the institution, those who fund it and society more generally, expect. Hopefully, such expectations should have some alignment to an ideal of good practice. How each new staff member goes about this, should, in broad terms, be left up to the individual. However, it is important that checks and support are in place to monitor progress so that the new staff member does what they are paid to do and is protected from exploitation. In many higher education systems this is conveniently determined by tenure processes, appraisal and promotion requirements. From outside the institution, academic work may be determined by professional bodies and by governments and funding agencies seeking accountability for the quality of teaching and research. If we consider external accountability important, then we can start to understand how to organize our activities as 'measurable' aspects of academic work.

In the broader context of accountability, the academic community should not feel compelled to invent new surveillance systems (such as workload models) as a proxy for transparency and fairness at work, or for correcting historically bad management practices (which I suspect have been the real driver for the widespread introduction of workload models). If academics were genuinely held to be responsible for the quality of their teaching and research, workload models would not be necessary. I do, however, recognize the intense pressure accountability and reward systems bring for individuals and also how this drives academics to be more competitive, in true neoliberal fashion. This competitiveness militates against collegiality and creates fertile ground for imaginative policies that are seen, at the very least, to manage other people's time.

Here are some thoughts on time management for the new academic. From day 1 in the job:

1   Teaching may demand your attention but research is the foundation of practice and the most valued (international) currency for a university career. Make sure you set aside at least a full day each week to do research because it requires extended time, especially for reading, writing and thinking.
2   Try not to volunteer for too much too soon. Your working week will fill up quickly regardless. Getting rid of responsibilities later is far harder than taking them on.
3   Be proactive as an apprentice academic and don't wait for others to 'invite you in'.
4   Make new contacts in your university outside your department and discipline because the internal and often closed world of the department does not reflect the possibilities for academic work.
5   Be constantly on the look out for income-generating opportunities.
6   Keep time for a private life and activities outside of academia.

You might be thinking that this list is remarkably small or perhaps that the issues are just not relevant, however, these six ideas have resonated with the majority of those I have worked with.

## A fair teaching load

Seeking a fair teaching load drives much of the debate around workloads. The amount of teaching one is asked to do is often determined when a job offer is made but the negotiation phase can be a vulnerable time for an academic. In an ideal world, both new and experienced lecturers would have a smaller load in their first year or two to allow a reasonable amount of time to get research established. It is a strategy that I have seen succeed well on a couple of occasions, but it is probably rare because in our mass higher education circumstances there is seldom spare capacity in the system that allows others to temporarily pick up teaching. There may also be no one else who teaches in a subject and such options are more difficult in small departments.

In direct contrast, a common observation made by the new lecturers I have worked with is that they were given a larger teaching load than their more established colleagues. Not only did they start with more direct contact hours but there was no consideration that courses needed to be designed from scratch or overhauled to fit new circumstances. How this situation occurs, I am not sure. There is some evidence that heads of departments try to protect their staff from this happening (Staniforth & Harland, 2006) because the consequences are that the working week gets extended while research is ignored. Either outcome seems unacceptable, but as argued in Chapter 7, concentrating on teaching and catching up on research later has career ramifications, especially if research productivity is measured and department funding (or survival) is contingent upon success.

## Problems with induction

Universities and departments do not always get induction right. Providing good support and timely information for a new staff member can be a big challenge, especially at department level, which is the main work site. If I had to summarize the experiences academics have shared with me, I would say that most were left to 'sink or swim' when they started work. Some were given poor guidance and a few ended up feeling not valued by departments or their university.

> And the head of department said ... of course we give academic staff a very good, thorough induction. And I was sitting there thinking: I've missed it. Where was it? When was it? And I said this to 'Neil' afterwards, the head of the research group, and he said: well you got the staff handbook.
> (Staniforth & Harland, 2006, p. 189)

Such issues suggest the academic community should be concerned about induction and the main problems that need to be addressed are listed in the table below:

*Table 8.1* Problems with induction (from Staniforth & Harland, 2006)

| Induction problem | Resolution |
| --- | --- |
| There was little or no meaningful communication between the new staff member and their head of department. | Regular meetings to discuss induction issues; have induction as a topic in programmes for training new departmental heads. |
| Even when heads understood induction, they did not ensure that it was done. | Each department requires reliable systems in place that take into account the individual and the different phases of induction. |
| There was no evaluation of induction experiences. | Use systematic evaluation to check on the staff member and the quality of the induction process. |
| New staff did not take initiative for their own induction. | Be proactive in getting information and in socialization; arrange for a mentor if one is not provided. |

Induction could be viewed as a collective social practice in which everyone in the community accepts some responsibility for ensuring a new staff member settles into work, although the process does need someone responsible to make sure that it happens and is successful. It has traditionally been the head of department who looks after a new staff member, but any established academic could take on this role.

## Academic freedom

We have now reached a position in higher education where academics are no longer trusted professionals and so must be accountable for all their work as new ways of governance and managing staff creep into our universities, and governments seek to erode the power of the sector. I have noted that such issues, important as they are to me, have not been of much interest to new academics.

Yet they have reported that compliance sets boundaries for their work and can help in decisions about what is valued and so create a reasonably 'level playing field' when it comes to tenure and promotion. An example of external compliance in New Zealand is the Performance-based Research Funding (PBRF) exercise, which holds every university teacher accountable to government for the quality of their research (note: university teachers are required by statute to be researchers). In the exercise, the range of research activities rewarded are specified by the government in great detail and we now have exactly the same criteria used in internal university tenure and promotion decisions.

When it comes to management, I have observed that it is easier to rely on policy and rules to enforce certain behaviours, rather than achieve control through interpersonal forms of communication. For example, if one academic abuses conference leave and funding by using the time for a holiday, the likely outcome is a new conference leave policy for everyone in order to prevent this happening again. Policy accountability is an attractive way of dealing with difficult staff-related issues, especially when the head of department rotates every three years or so, and organizational memory is lost. In such systems each new head is usually a senior academic with limited expertise in management who is aware they will go back to the ranks and join those they supervised after their term of office. This is not an easy situation for anyone. In more hierarchical systems of department organization and those with permanent chairs, such problems lessen as new academics are treated less like peers and more like subordinates.

There are always pros and cons to any form of accountability but the pros tend to give the impression that each exercise is 'reasonable'. However, being held accountable for certain academic activities has the unfortunate consequence of marginalizing others. In particular our freedom to provide a wide range of services to society seems to be threatened. In a survey of academic work in a UK university just over 3 per cent of academics' time was spent on external activities, while research, teaching and administration accounted for 87 per cent (Staniforth & Harland, 1999). Bruce Macfarlane claims the 'the role of service has been, by and large, overlooked or trivialized as little more than 'administration' rather than essential to the preservation of community life' (Macfarlane, 2005, p. 299). If this analysis is correct and reflective of higher education more widely, it calls into question whether or not universities really do have a wide service role to play in society and, if there is no explicit reward for and recognition of service to signal its importance to academic work, will it be further marginalized as pressures increase on other aspects of academic work? Macfarlane argues, however, that academic commitment to service has never been just about financial rewards and he suggests responsibility for its survival may lie in the actions of senior academics acting as role models. I feel, however, that both academic freedom and our service to students and society are diminished by accountability and much time can be wasted on exercises that provide no outcomes beyond form filling for a hollow kind of bureaucracy.

## Thoughts for reflection

1 The average working week for an academic is about 50 hours and this has not changed much over the last 40 years (Tight, 2010), despite the move to mass higher education across the world in the 1980s and 1990s. Tight argues that such a working week is what is feasible or tolerable. I would like to think it represents the 'saturation limit' for the type of work academics do.

2 A way of managing workload issues is to assume that academics will always try to protect their research first, because this is the most valued of all activities, and then build all other work around a fixed period of research. Then, to ensure transparency and equity in departments, academics have regular conversations with colleagues to chat about what is going on in their practice. An open and informal strategy will lesson anxiety about fairness in workloads and is likely to have other socialization benefits.

3 Before applying for your next academic post, do some careful research into the prospective university, department and its staff. It never ceases to amaze me, especially when this information is easily accessible, how many new academics did none of this before accepting a contract. In

addition, I have observed that some newly appointed junior academics have been poor at negotiating pay and conditions and so spend the early part of a new job feeling resentment towards their head of department (who usually does the negotiation) or towards their colleagues because of what they come to realize as comparably unfair terms of employment. I can think of no worse start to a career and it seems beyond belief that a department or faculty would deliberately seek to create such conditions. I would like to think that when this happens it is a symptom of amateur management practices or lack of thought, rather than lack of care or an attempt to exploit new staff. If you are reading this as an established academic please do not forget your own experiences of starting work when the next recruitment exercise comes along in your department. What contribution will you make to the process?

4    Academics take different routes into higher education and the roles they play are wide-ranging. This complexity takes some getting used to when starting out, even though there is still a common understanding of the core tasks of the profession. Academics research and teach and contribute to administration and service. However, this core, still evident in the older humanities and science disciplines, may not hold in professional education settings, such as medicine, law or commerce, or in some of the newer disciplines that have found a place in our universities. Such institutional diversity may seem irrelevant to a new academic, whose initial world is their subject and department. However, getting to know what is happening across an institution or sector can change thinking and open up a vast range of possibilities for academic work. Academics may no longer be engaged in traditional roles and can have major responsibilities in areas such as income generation, commercial development of intellectual capital and professional education. How should we celebrate this diversity? How do we avoid creating subordinate minorities within our universities?

## References

Austin, A.E. (2002) Creating a bridge to the future: Preparing new faculty to face changing expectations in a shifting context, *The Review of Higher Education*, 26(2), 119–44.

Macfarlane, B. (2005) The disengaged academic: The retreat from citizenship, *Higher Education Quarterly*, 59(4), 296–312.

Staniforth, D. & Harland, T. (1999) The work of an academic: Jack of all trades, or master of one? *International Journal for Academic Development*, 4(2), 142–9.

——(2006) Contrasting views of induction: The experiences of new academic staff and their heads of department, *Active Learning in Higher Education*, 7(2), 185–96.

Tight, M. (2010) Are academic workloads increasing? The postwar survey evidence in the UK, *Higher Education Quarterly*, 64(2), 200–15.

## Further reading

Schuster, J.H. & Finkelstein, M.J. (2006) *The American faculty: The restructuring of academic work and careers*, Baltimore: The John Hopkins University Press.

Tennant, M., McMullen, C. & Kaczynski, D. (2010) *Teaching, learning and research in higher education: A critical approach*, New York: Routledge.

# Field note 8
## Collegial departments and the exercise of power

Reaching a decision or implementing change can seem interminably slow in a collegiate department. It is said that this is the cost of a democratic workplace where collective expertise is valued. I am particularly interested in what I have come to think of as the exercise of 'negative power' (with apologies to Foucault, 2000). I often see this played out in various settings such as staff and planning meetings, committees and so on. Academics in a collegial situation are accustomed to using their intellect for evaluating the merit of ideas and then giving their opinions, making suggestions and pointing out alternatives. However, contributions can also be quite disabling should debate cultivate a situation that creates enough inertia to render decisions too hard to make, timely action more difficult and for other staff to feel subordinated.

I have observed this phenomenon in many situations and do not think it is typically a malicious act; rather, it is enacted subconsciously and can come about with the best of intentions. A key problem in claiming that such exercise is negative is that the play of power in critical debate is typically experienced as positive, necessary and helpful. Moreover, it often appears reasonable: have you thought of this ... we may need to include such and such ... you can't do it that way ... what about ... ?, and so on.

However, such debate, especially in a setting without a strong chair, can result in individuals losing ownership of ideas and becoming less motivated, in particular when the process is prolonged with further meetings and negotiation until 'we get it right'. Innovation tends to come from individuals and the 'we' in these situations is often a group of individuals who have different levels of investment in a project but a belief that they should be consulted and have their ideas taken seriously. In my argument, these colleagues feel they are being positive but they often have little insight into the impact of their contribution. If their actions have a negative impact that subordinates or alienates others, then this is the exercise of negative power. If we do not get these social-professional situations right, then there is the natural temptation to move from collegial work structures to a managerial culture that uses bureaucratic and hierarchical systems to give some protection against the abuse of power. However, for those with a strong value for collegiality, much is then lost, including personal autonomy, power and motivation to take risks and innovate. Collegiality calls for insight into our own behaviours, motives and values and a deep understanding of the needs of those we work with.

Foucault, M. (2000) Power, In J.D. Faubion (ed.), Essential Works of Foucault, Volume 3, New York: The New York Press

# Chapter 9

# The purposes and values of a university education

## Introduction

This chapter is concerned with the question of what we are trying to achieve with academic work, or more specifically, how we might comprehend the purposes of a university education and enact the values that inform our understanding (Harland & Pickering, 2011). Of course there are many purposes and any response will depend on conceptions of academic work, subject and discipline, stage of career and also on philosophical considerations concerning what an academic thinks their university and society asks of them. I argue that to appreciate what can be achieved in teaching and academic work requires a systematic exploration of our ideas about what constitutes a university education.

In my conversations with early career academics I typically find fairly restricted ideas about what they are seeking to achieve with their work. As a consequence, they have limited objectives in both teaching and research. This situation is not surprising given their lack of experience coupled with the immediate demands of starting a new job. As a general observation, I would contend that beyond the creation and dissemination of subject knowledge the majority have not had enough time to consider their broader responsibilities towards students and society, or what constitutes a university education that is 'higher' in some way. I maintain that narrow conceptions necessarily limit practice and because the collective academic community shapes the university, individuals are ultimately responsible for the university's responses to knowledge and society. If this analysis is correct, then the question of purposes should be considered sooner rather than later because any answers will shape a career from the earliest point.

It is not only the new lecturer who has the task of working out the purposes of academic work and it is not unusual to find more experienced academics who confidently assert that it is not their responsibility to go beyond research and teaching in a subject and a clear discipline-knowledge boundary. If you compare such conceptions with those of the university, there will be a difference in expectations. Any statement around graduate attributes will include outcomes around knowledge, skills, attitudes and values. It could be argued that in some cases, the employer is asking for certain outcomes while the employee has other ideas in mind, and that collegial work structures and ideas about academic freedom allow for the possibility of such a situation. The sceptic might observe that there is a convenient silence on this disparity or that mission statements are just tokenistic. I contend that because academics genuinely have a lot of freedom in what they choose to do, they also have a responsibility to justify the choices they make. They can ignore or deny practice elements at their convenience but in doing so they risk living with and enacting a narrow conception of both academic work and university education.

To encourage a broader dialogue on the potential of university teaching, I offer some views about higher education expressed by different stakeholders. In doing so I hope to introduce a range of possibilities that go beyond knowledge creation and dissemination and contribute to a theory of purposes.

## The students' view

The students I interviewed were able to articulate their thoughts about purposes with ease, which suggests they had carefully considered the matter since graduating. A range of responses were given and I have placed these in five categories and then ranked them in order of the number of students who shared an idea:

*Table 9.1* The purposes of a university education. Twenty-four graduates were asked what the purposes of a university education were. N = number of students who expressed ideas within each of five main categories. Categories are ranked in order of importance

| The purposes of a university education | Rank | Student responses that illustrate the concept |
| --- | --- | --- |
| Personal intellectual development | 1 (N=23) | Being able to question, evaluate, think critically, see the world in a different way, advance knowledge. |
| Skills training | 2 (N=6) | Having knowledge and skills. Relevant education for work. |
| Personal growth | 3 (N=5) | Being able to apply oneself, to be self-motivated, know how to learn and take responsibility for it. |
| Socialization | 4 (N=3) | Understanding how to learn from others and learning to live with others. |
| Being productive in society | 5 (N=2) | Using the benefits of education to contribute to society. How to live better lives. |

If this small group of New Zealand (NZ) university-educated students is representative of a wider body of learners, then higher education could be said to be in reasonably good health (if purposes are played out in practice). Prior to the study I would have predicted that knowledge and skills training would have been the highest priority rather than the critical dimensions of education. These responses also seem to contrast with the view that contemporary universities are mainly about producing workers for economic gain.

Only one graduate started their explanation of purposes by talking about social goals. They expressed these in the context of being 'productive in society'. However, later in the interview all 24 were asked specifically what they thought society gained from their education. It was put to them that society invests in them financially and so might reasonably expect something in return for this support. It is fair to say that most struggled with this question and for those who had left NZ after completing their degree, a sense of guilt was clearly evident. One overseas respondent could not articulate his contribution to society but with regards to his university education he thanked 'the NZ public for paying for most of it'. Another suggested 'the benefit to society is that the individual gets a highly paid job'. The remaining students saw both positive and negative effects on society and described these as follows:

*Table 9.2* Students' ideas about positive and negative impacts of a university education on society

| *Positive impact* | *Negative impact* |
| --- | --- |
| Creating knowledge for society. | Creates an under-class of people without degrees. |
| Contributes to the economy which benefits everyone. | A university education is seen as a commodity. |
| Allows for society to do things better. | Produces one big 'old boys club' for graduates (also seen as positive by others). |
| Knowledge can be critiqued. Transmitting the values of education to family and others. | |
| Obtain a questioning society that protects democracy. | |
| Graduates have the credibility to comment on issues. | |

Another respondent used the phrase 'critic and conscience of society' and in NZ it can be argued that all academics and students should provide such a service, not least because this university requirement is enshrined in the current Education Act (see 'A societal view' below). The idea of being a critic of and for society was also supported in the study but there was a caveat. Several students reflected that they had a lot more freedom to exercise criticism while at university, but in the workforce, freedoms had been 'taken away'. It was suggested that universities are more open than other societal institutions but that with greater commercialization of university activities, such a position was under threat. Finally, one graduate suggested that contributions to society are often hard to see but quite easy to justify historically.

## The new lecturer's view

I have a field notebook entry that I made in February 2004. I was writing about one of the first discussions I had with an academic about the purposes of a higher education. In this case it was with a highly successful and respected colleague from science. It was obvious from our conversation that he had not given the idea much thought, beyond the notion of doing high-quality research and teaching. I wrote that 'the concept does not seem to have much relevance ... ', but also noted that there were also barriers of language and meaning at play with respect to our ideas about responsibilities. For example, he claimed that: 'questions of purpose are more relevant to your field of higher education' (rather than to the discipline he worked in).

My colleague's remarks made an impact on my thinking and I have since been curious to explore the question of aims and purposes with others, especially the new academics I work with. It think it is fair to say that most pay a lot of attention to aspects of research, teaching and academic life, but nearly all thinking is restricted, given the possibilities for higher education and the various roles a university can play in society. If I had to make a generalization, those new to academic life start with a narrow view of practice and at best gradually develop ideas over a very long period of time, nearly exclusively within the context of disciplinary knowledge and skills. Research purposes are typically explained in terms of knowledge creation and applied utility, and teaching and learning is about acquiring sound subject knowledge and skills. Yet there is much more that can be achieved and to understand this we ought to at least explore the range of possibilities for our work. By asking what is appropriate for a university education, and then which ideas are more important, new thoughts will challenge us. Should any have genuine value, practice will change (see 'A higher education view' below).

## The university view

The mission statements and teaching plans of each university usually provide an interesting and well-thought-out account of aims and purposes. The more comprehensive of these should cause an academic to reflect on what they are doing, but translating institutional goals into personal guides for action seems to be fraught with a long history of failure. The first barrier is that new academics simply do not read institutional documents and, if they do, they find the contents rather abstract with little immediate relevance to the demands of work. Even sensible summaries of what good teaching looks like do not seem to influence academic practice.

Documents that contain statements of purpose can also seem far removed from daily life and what may be more influential are the values enacted by the institution's leaders and close colleagues, and, of course, the reward structures that determine academic success. However, leaders are often invisible and reward structures will inevitably focus on a narrow set of measurable outcomes that will represent only a fraction of the possibilities that are typically included in university plans or mission statements.

## A societal view

Here I use the term society in the narrow context of legislation and the NZ government's efforts on behalf of its citizens. The following characteristics of a university are specified in the Education Act (1989):

  I  They are primarily concerned with more advanced learning, the principal aim being to develop intellectual independence.
 II  Their research and teaching are closely interdependent and most of their teaching is done by people who are active in advancing knowledge.
III  They meet international standards of research and teaching.
 IV  They are a repository of knowledge and expertise.
  V  They accept a role as critic and conscience of society.

The first four conditions are not surprising but New Zealand is unique in embedding the received idea of 'critic and conscience' in law. This situation, however, presents academics with the difficult challenge of accepting such a responsibility and putting it into practice. My colleagues and I (Harland *et al.*, 2010) have argued that if a conscience is an internal voice that reflects our ability to distinguish between right and wrong, then this becomes the foundation of our moral values. Developing such moral values requires the ability to reason and being critical in this process requires a conscience, if we accept the position that our reasoning and actions always depend on our values. In our research we concluded that the Education Act (V) does not charge academics to accept two tasks, but a single task in that we have to be both 'critic *and* conscience' at the same time:

> If you want to be critic and conscience of society, it's about having an awareness of what that society is doing and having the ability to critique it and then developing some sort of attitude towards it, some sort of conscience.
>
> (Harland *et al.*, 2010, p. 93)

We also need to be aware of how our ideas and actions are used in society and we might call this a 'downstream' notion of conscience. In this context, conscience-type activities seem to be more obvious in certain disciplines, for example, moral philosophy compared with food science, and in some educational systems, for example, post-apartheid South Africa and New Zealand. Yet all academics need to work out the moral foundations of their thinking and how their choices and actions might impact on society because these are realized in our normal disciplinary teaching and research activities as well as in our service roles. Almost a hundred years ago John Dewey (1916) suggested that academics should not give society lessons in morals but should acknowledge that how they conduct themselves and live their academic values has broader social implications. In all the actions of the university, its staff and its students we are 'critic and conscience of society' and this should be taken seriously.

## A higher education view

Is there anything universal in how academics might understand their role and that of the university? Universities have something unique to contribute to society and Ron Barnett, in 'The idea of higher education' (Barnett, 1990) argues that academics are in remarkable agreement about the sorts of things higher education can provide. He describes these as a cluster of aims, values and general ideas and he offers the following (not exhaustive) list:

- the pursuit of truth and objective knowledge;
- research;
- liberal education;
- institutional autonomy;
- academic freedom;
- a neutral and open forum for debate;
- rationality;
- the development of the student's critical abilities;
- the development of the student's autonomy;

- the student's character formation;
- providing a critical centre within society;
- preserving society's intellectual culture.

(Barnett, 1990, pp. 8–9)

We may agree (or not) with these ideas, or see them as just another type of mission statement. However, if they really do describe academic practice, then realizing them is likely to be a challenge for most academics in the majority of disciplines. For new staff, in particular, there are pressing requirements that will take precedent. The luxury of settling into university life with, for example, a half-time teaching load and a long-term view of establishing research, may belong to another era. The more liberal ideas about a contemplative academic life have been seriously undermined by the contemporary changes to higher education that started with the neoliberal political reforms of the early 1980s (Chapter 6). Although these have yet to fully play out, they have changed the nature of academic work.

One of the main impacts of neoliberalism has been the move to mass or near-universal higher education in many parts of the world (Shattock, 2010). At the same time, at least in the Western liberal public sectors, governments have insisted on greater economic efficiencies, less reliance on state funding and new measures of accountability. Staff–student ratios continue to increase (at least in the successful subjects and in those institutions in demand) and these changes challenge how we go about research, teaching and being an academic in a competitive marketplace. It has certainly created a pressured academic community and made it more difficult to identify what now constitutes a higher education and what is possible for our universities that now find themselves key players in the new knowledge economies.

With respect to teaching, we appear to have reached a situation in which we can only serve the majority of students if we provide something less than we know is possible. If an academic has worked throughout the recent reforms, they are certain to claim that the majority of students are not provided for as well as we might wish. Quality, however, is not lost entirely. Even though we open up higher education to increasing numbers, our 'top' students are never ignored because we need to maintain our knowledge fields through the next generation of researchers. The elite nature of higher education is preserved for a small number who receive an education that genuinely realizes their full potential. The larger student body receives something else.

Some suggest we consciously 'dumb down' but this charge seems unfair, as few would intentionally seek to provide a lower standard of education. However, the impact of neoliberal reform has contributed to a shift in how we measure achievement. For example, the award of a first class degree or high grade point average (GPA) is much more common while there is no evidence that students are studying more or that levels of intelligence have changed (Tucker & Courts, 2010). Furthermore, the current global economic downturn and so-called 'period of austerity' has resulted in a university degree no longer guaranteeing employment (Shattock, 2010). In a number of professional work situations a Masters or PhD has replaced a first-degree qualification while at the same time, many postgraduates can no longer find work. The overall effect of recent reform has been to alter how we understand our qualifications and what is possible to achieve in our mass education system. Academics know that opportunities to educate students at the highest possible level remain and losing sight of this imperils universities as the guardians of quality and gatekeepers of educational standards. Any articulation of purposes will need to take into account these issues.

## Conclusions

In this chapter I have used stakeholder views to illustrate a case for all academics to continually question their work in order to develop a personal philosophy of higher education that will, in due course, translate into a practical set of aims for research, teaching and service, first in the discipline and then for the university and higher education. I recognize that such an exercise needs to take the form of a long-term inquiry that examines both practice and beliefs and also takes into account the views of those who have an interest in higher education. However, a start can be made by carefully reflecting on existing tacit knowledge and trying to make this more explicit (Chapter 1). Academics will probably find they are already fulfilling countless outcomes and realizing purposes they had not thought about or had not consciously set out to achieve.

Students have always had very different strengths, abilities and motivation to learn. For those who might not wish to, or be able to take advantage of the educational opportunities on offer, what do we now provide? The problem seems to be more and more students occupying some 'middle' ground. Whereas motivated high achievers can still access the best that universities have to offer, and others leave when they decide a higher education is not for them, the majority seem to take up some intermediate position, and as yet we are not sure how to fully provide for them. In this mass higher-education situation, a challenge for academics is to work out how they develop a clear set of purposes for as many students as possible, without sacrificing excellence.

## Thoughts for reflection

Are there general principles to guide an inquiry into purposes? If we take into account the views of the different stakeholders I have outlined above, there might be agreement about the following ideas:

1   A higher education is more than knowledge and skills (even in applied and professional courses).
2   Each student must to be able to take their place in society as more than an economic resource. Being educated and prepared for work and a career is of paramount importance but it cannot be the sole purpose of a university education.
3   That every student is given the opportunity to reach their full potential.

And in trying to realize these aspirations, academics must have the appropriate resources.

There are others principles that may appear more contentious with respect to our common understanding of educational purposes. I believe these to sit on the periphery of mainstream thinking about academic practice:

1   There is freedom to learn for students and because higher education is the learner's responsibility, there is also freedom to fail.
2   Universities remain one of the few societal institutions that still play a pivotal and privileged role in maintaining democratic systems of government and society.
3   That students will take their place in society and make a difference, for better or worse, and universities must accept their part in this.
4   That all university education teaches students values, whether or not this is done consciously or by default.

## References

Barnett, R. (1990) *The idea of higher education*, Buckingham: Society for Research in Higher Education and Open University Press.

Dewey, J. (1916) *Democracy and education*, New York: The Macmillan Company.

Education Act Amendment (1989) *Part 14 Establishment and disestablishment of tertiary institutions*, S162, 4(a)(v), New Zealand Government.

Harland, T. & Pickering, N. (2011) *Values in higher education teaching*, London: Routledge.

Harland, T., Tidswell, T. Everett, D., Hale, L. & Pickering, N. (2010) Neoliberalism and the academic as critic and conscience of society, *Teaching in Higher Education*, 15(1), 85–96.

Shattock, M. (2010) Managing mass higher education in a period of austerity, *Arts and Humanities in Higher Education*, 9(1), 22–30.

Tucker, J. & Courts, B. (2010) Grade inflation in the college classroom, *Foresight*, 12(1): 45–53.

## Further reading

Barnett, R. (2003) *Beyond all reason: Living with ideology in the university*, Buckingham: Society for Research in Higher Education and Open University Press.

Rowland, S. (2006) *The enquiring university: Compliance and contestation in higher education*, Maidenhead: Open University Press, McGraw-Hill Education.

# Field note 9
## Liberal educational values
- - - - - - - - - - - - - - - - - - - -

Liberal educational values have been a part of the modern university for so long and they still underpin research. It is difficult to imagine these values completely marginalized. Similarly, it is not easy to see how a research academic could set one standard of thinking for herself in her research and another for her teaching. The cycle of academic renewal would be broken in a single generation of students. Because we understand what it is to be an academic, we ensure these ideas are passed down to those who follow us.

There is, however, a danger in losing integrity if our version of academic life is narrow and constrained. At all times, academic practice should be seen as contestable and open to intellectual inquiry. Yet there must also be a reason why academics would invest in such an idea. Why take a risk and put time and energy into understanding the project and values of a university?

# Chapter 10

# The subject and the idea
# of critical thinking

## Introduction

Although students come to university to study a subject, their learning and experiences go way beyond this. Similarly, when a new lecturer starts thinking about how to teach their subject, they will start with factual and theoretical forms of knowledge and gradually become more focused on other dimensions of learning as they develop new ideas about the wider purposes of education and what they want students to accomplish. There are many ways of learning in a subject that lead to very different outcomes. For example, teaching that is concerned primarily with the development of the intellect will have its own characteristics and will contrast with teaching that emphasizes the accumulation of factual knowledge. Knowing a lot about a subject is an important characteristic of a graduate, as is a good memory, but we also expect them to acquire a wide range of cognitive and practical skills and a certain quality of mind. Determining what is of most value for a student's education is certain to require a repertoire of appropriate teaching strategies.

For the university teacher who wants to go beyond subject knowledge, perhaps the most important single consideration is critical thinking. This concept has almost universal support at a theoretical and emotional level and so provides the perfect starting point and guide for organizing teaching and curricular practices (Wass *et al.*, 2011). To be able to think critically within a body of knowledge allows for challenge, progress and the development of new ideas. Learning a body of knowledge using a critical approach can transform that knowledge and thinking. Critical thought then becomes part of the reflexivity inherent in each discipline that allows the field to advance (Barnett, 1997), and in turn the field becomes an important vehicle for developing critical thought. Such an outcome also has implications beyond the subject and discipline as learners can apply thinking skills and a critical disposition to many other problems of an intellectual and practical character. It is hard to imagine a graduate student who has developed as an accomplished critical thinker being able to consciously shut down their intellectual skills after they leave university. If this assertion is correct, then critical thinking is for life and we set students on a journey that is not easily reversed.

In this chapter, I introduce some ideas about critical thinking and how we might help students to become critical thinkers. As part of this topic, I will consider assessment, from the perspectives of both assessing

---

**Critical Thinking Quiz**

I have a working definition of critical thinking
YES/NO
This is (could be):

_____

_____

_____

In my course documentation the written learning objectives include statements
and criteria about critical thinking
YES/NO
An example is (could be):

_____

_____

_____

In group work I have strategies that allow students space in which they can
rehearse critical thinking
YES/NO
An example is (could be):

_____

_____

_____

In my assessments of student learning, the students know that I always reward
critical thinking
YES/NO
I do this by (I would like to do this by):

_____

_____

_____

After my students have graduated from university, I am confident that they will
be critical thinkers
YES/NO
My evidence for this belief is (could be):

_____

_____

_____

---

*Figure 10.1* Critical thinking quiz

student's critical thinking and taking a critical look at current assessment practices. Before you read on, please complete the critical thinking quiz on page 107.

## Critical thinking

There is wide agreement that critical thinking is foundational to university education (Barnett, 1997). Academics not only embody this value in much of their own work but also seek it for their students. Because critical thinking is a defining concept of a higher education it is a good subject for the teacher who would like to move beyond the idea of teaching factual knowledge and instrumental skills. Rather than ask what you want students to know, the question becomes 'What does it mean to be a critical thinker in, say, zoology (or history, or medicine, and so on)?' and then, 'How do I help my students become critical thinkers in my discipline?'

### What does it mean to be a critical thinker?

At university, critical thinking is developed by a student in the social context of learning in their discipline. It is learnt through studying a subject and it is not something that can be developed independently of this. It can be applied to new areas of interest but these, too, contain a subject. Critical thinking is usually thought of either in terms of a skill or as a special way of thinking. As such, it embodies the qualities we would normally associate with the university researcher. Pascarella & Terenzini (1991) have suggested a critical thinker should be able to:

- identify the central issues in an argument;
- recognize important relationships;
- make correct inferences from data;
- deduce conclusions from the data;
- interpret whether or not the conclusion are warranted on the basis of the data;
- evaluate evidence.

But as a 'way of thinking' a student would display certain dispositions and be:

- habitually inquisitive;
- well-informed;

- fair-minded in evaluation;
- trustful of reason;
- honest in facing personal biases;
- prudent in making judgements;
- willing to reconsider.

(Facione, 1990)

These two lists seem different but both illustrate how we might understand critical thinking. They are not extensive and are included here as an example of the sorts of ideas embodied in the concept to help the teacher of critical thinking decide what they might aim for and what they would then need to assess. Overall the task is to provide opportunities for the student to think in alternative ways and to have new thoughts and these ought to be required for all courses and programmes in a university.

### How do I help my students become critical thinkers in my discipline?

If you want a simple teaching strategy for critical thinking, then train students to be researchers. Authentic research requires a critical mind at each stage of the process, from formulating questions, gathering data, analysis of evidence and writing up. Knowledge of the research subject is a key part of this process and factual forms of knowledge are used and learnt in the context of inquiry. Writing up is vital to critical thought because it is through this process that thinking can be examined and re-evaluated in the drafting and redrafting of an essay or report.

This idea is not novel *per se* and many universities organize programmes with a final-year honours research project as a capstone experience. However, there is a repeated pattern across the sector of large first-year classes that focus on learning basic foundational knowledge (particularly in science and health science subjects) and then at the later stages of the undergraduate degree, of smaller specialized programmes that focus on research skills. Part of the developmental argument for this step-wise experience is that students need good factual subject knowledge so that they will have something to think critically about later.

Perhaps less common is to have students doing research from the first day they enter university, yet this is where a focus on critical thinking ought to start. One reason why we might seek this early is that if our ultimate aim is to develop a critical disposition in students, then this takes considerable time. Students need to practise critical thinking so they feel comfortable and confident in using thinking skills both inside and outside their disciplinary context. Doing authentic research and learning to both 'think and act' like a researcher, will take most students a long way towards these goals.

To provide an education of this type for first-year students requires the university lecturer to teach in a similar manner to a postgraduate research supervisor and reframe their methods and practices accordingly. Such a curriculum structure would of necessity need more time apportioned for student research and less time would be available for acquiring other forms of basic knowledge. I am not suggesting that all of a student's university education can or should be organized as a series of research projects, but would advocate that at any time a student is studying at a university, they should be engaged in some form of research. They can then bring their new-found critical abilities to bear on all other curriculum experiences. However, the more they do research, the greater the benefit to higher-order thinking. Gradually building towards a final-year research project is not enough and students are capable of carrying out original work in their subject as soon as they enter university.

## Critical assessment

Any enthusiast for critical thinking will have to address the question of assessment. Assessment is termed summative when we assess students and then award a mark or grade, and formative when we make evaluative judgements with the objective of helping students improve as learners. In practice, the boundaries between summative or formative assessment are not discrete but it is a helpful distinction because of the impact the grading process has on student behaviour. Students all want to 'pass' and some want to get good grades; all are acutely aware that so much in their future depends on the marks they are awarded.

Grading critical thinking in the context of thinking skills or dispositions can be idiosyncratic and unreliable because of the difficulties in describing what it is we expect from students. Although critical thinking is a defining concept of higher education, defining what it means is not easy. This problem is particularly acute when standards of judgement need to be shared among groups of academics so that assessment fulfils its purpose of grading students fairly. What we expect students to learn can be assessed without much difficulty when we ask for recall of factual knowledge and principles, but for critical thinking, the statements describing it are open to interpretation. For example, what permits a marker to award a low or high grade for being critical of the central issue in an argument or for showing prudent judgement? We need to be able to recognize good critical thinking as opposed to weak critical thinking.

Instead of seeking inter-marker consistency and reliability, markers need to justify decisions in terms of validity as they align what they want students to learn with assessment practices. In other words, is the assessment fit for its purposes? Personal judgement about standards is crucial and, with respect to critical thinking, experienced lecturers will claim that they 'know it when they see it' and can reward it appropriately. I do not doubt that this claim has a lot of truth in it, but assertions of this nature seem very out of place in today's universities.

What teachers can do to be even-handed with students is develop dialogue around critical thinking and its assessment with colleagues, especially those they are teaching with. Try to come to some agreed notion of standards and purposes. It is unlikely to be perfect or totally reliable but examples of students' past work, model answers written by experienced academics (e.g. research essays, reports) and double marking can help in these tasks. Assessment of many worthwhile objectives will never be truly objective but academics can learn to recognize and reward good thinking, tell students apart and gain some insight into the impact that their teaching has on student learning and development.

With respect to critical thinking, Bloom's *Taxonomy of educational objectives* (Bloom *et al.*, 1956) can help the new teacher in determining what to teach, how to teach it and how to grade it (Biggs & Tang, 2007, Chapter 5). Amongst other goals, Bloom wanted to create educational objectives that would allow meaning to be shared between different markers while describing the range of educational possibilities for learning. He created a set of categories thought to show a step-wise progression from simple to more complex learning objectives. Krathwohl (2002) revised the original categories and for the cognitive domain these can be summarized as:

*Table 10.1* Verbs for learning objectives derived from Bloom's Taxonomy

| Categories | For example |
| --- | --- |
| Remember | Retrieving knowledge from memory |
| Understand | Determining the meaning of information |
| Apply | Applying knowledge to a situation |
| Analyse | Analysing elements and determining relationships |
| Evaluate | Making a judgement based on criteria |
| Create | Producing an original product |

Application, analysis, evaluation and creation all tend to require some higher-order thinking and so can be used as a guide for the new teacher as they learn to write objectives and assessment items for critical thinking. As a starting point, include the required category as a verb in each objective. Writing an assessment item for a particular objective in this way ensures the teacher is explicit in their expectations for student learning and will align assessment with teaching purpose.

However useful this strategy may be, I am not convinced that learning necessarily takes place in a step-wise manner or that it will help different markers share views on the difference between a good and not so good 'analysis', 'evaluation' or 'original product'. In addition, these thinking skills often need to be complemented by the affective domain that includes values (for example, how we feel about something) and the practical domain (for example, performing a complex hands-on task) and these will depend on subject and discipline.

## Making assessment practices critical

It is easy to see why university teachers have to make sure critical thinking assessment practices are critical in themselves. It would be hard to live with the idea of assessing critical thinking in a non-critical manner and I examine this idea in the context of:

1   the impact of assessment on student behaviour;
2   the decisions teachers make in what they choose to assess.

It seems reasonable that students will direct their efforts where they are rewarded most. So it is also reasonable that all summative assessment (of tasks that carry marks) address the most important learning outcomes we desire, including, when appropriate, the various dimensions of critical thinking. To determine which outcomes are assessed requires a critical decision by the lecturer because there must always be an inclination to assess what is seen as 'easy' or 'practical', rather than what is important and what we genuinely value. Assessing the factual content of a subject through recall tends to be relatively straightforward when compared to something like assessing the application of knowledge in a new situation.

If assessment practices need to be critical, you might ask what 'un-critical' practices might consist of. Here are a few ideas around in-course (internal) summative assessment. They all appear detrimental in some way to critical thinking and to learning more generally. Some may sound a little far-fetched but I have observed each of the practices described in the following table:

*Table 10.2* Un-critical assessment

| Un-critical assessment | Features |
| --- | --- |
| Any assessment given without knowledge of all the other assessments required of a student at that time. | Students on your course often have other assessment commitments and these can coincide or all come so close together that the student is forced into organizing limited time and effort around these tasks. Often this results in skipping lectures and tutorials to buy time, or cutting corners to get through. |
| Assessment patterns that drive student learning. | Frequent in-course assessments that carry a very small percentage of the overall grade. Students spend much their university life going from one test to another as they work for a few marks that all add up in the end. Assessment now drives all learning. |
| Assessments that focus on what is easy to grade rather than what is desirable. | It is much easier to assess objective forms of knowledge but hard to even define the parameters and content of something like 'critical thinking'. |
| Assessments that do not seek to assess critical thinking. | Academics 'know' when they see critical thinking but describing it for students in terms of a testable criterion is fraught with difficulty. |
| Using assessment to control behaviour. | If we do not assess the work, then the students will not do it. Courses are not independent of each other and if another gives marks for an assignment, the students will put their effort in that direction. To pull them back to work on our course we make a counter-offer of an assessment that also carries marks. |

Some of these ideas about in-course assessment tasks also hold for mid-term and final exams, and they reflect the difficulties experienced when a lecturer wants to assess something like critical thinking, while the overall assessment regime is antithetical to this. In our mass higher-education systems we have moved away from the practice of using only a final exam to regimes that include much more in-course assessment. The concern with this change is that we can end up 'over-assessing' students (in this argument I am only focusing on summative assessment). Over-assessment is likely to be detrimental to a higher education and critical thinking when the student no longer has any space left for self-determination in their learning because all their efforts are directed towards responding to a range of small tasks that are graded or marked. What is worthwhile becomes 'What's it worth?' and 'What's in it for me?' (see Barnett, 2003, p. 123).

What I would like to propose is that we have less in-course summative assessment tasks and put more emphasis on assessing larger assignments such as research-based projects or essays that take time and integrate and test higher-order learning categories. Students will need reasonable periods of time to do these well. We could also re-examine and increase the value of the final exam, although such a move will seem anti-educational to many because it suggests a return to what is often seen as a discredited practice.

Yet reliance on exams may not be such a bad idea in certain circumstances. By and large, higher education has replaced the stress of one final examination with the stress of multiple in-course assessments on top of a smaller exam. We have substituted one intense period of revision with the anxiety that comes from an insidious trickle of small assessments. Contemporary students always seem to have assessment on their mind, whether or not there is an assignment due, an online test to do, an essay, a short mid-term test, a laboratory check-out test and so on. At least the final exam was something that had to be dealt with sometime in the future and this allowed students more space and freedom to study as they wished until that time. They also knew that they would have to relearn everything in that semester or year before the exam, and this took the pressure off them for a while. The final exam contrasts markedly with a strategy of continually assessing small chunks of knowledge in a short space of time where it is learnt or mastered once and then typically fades as the next assessment looms.

I have no doubt that the final exam favours those with strong coping mechanisms and good memories, and there is clear evidence that students prefer in-course assessment as they can accumulate marks and get a sense of how well they are doing as they go (Trotter, 2006). Yet in a modular mass higher-education system, the whole of a student's learning experience can be framed by the test, always having an assessment to force learning, rather than learn through personal motivation and intellectual curiosity. I have heard lecturers argue that they use in-course assessment to 'make' students study. Apparently they will not do the work if there are no marks attached and Trotter's study on student perceptions of summative assessment supports this: students prefer to be made to work. The assumption here seems to be that it is the teacher's responsibility to ensure their students study and learn.

So we now have a university experience in which students are caught up from day one working for the test and this culture will be hard to change. If you take away internal assessments in one course, then the students will simply put effort into another where marks are at stake. To assess less or differently will require a shift across an institution or programme if the

*Table 10.3* Extract from an interview with two second-year students about assessment

| | |
|---|---|
| Interviewer: | Why do you feel unhappy with assessment? |
| Student 1: | Because we are always doing an assessment. There has never been a time at university when I have not been working for an assessment that counts. |
| Interviewer: | What do you mean by 'counts'? |
| Student 1: | Something that carries a mark towards my final grade. |
| Interviewer: | How often are you assessed in this way? |
| Student 1: | Probably every few days, certainly twice a week. I am only taking three courses this semester and I feel like I am being continuously assessed. |
| Interviewer: | What would you rather see happen? |
| Student 1: | I don't know, but I always thought that when I came to university it would be different to high school and I could do some of my own reading. I have been so busy this last year and a half that I have never had any opportunity. |
| Student 2: | I don't mind the assessments but I wish they did not all come at once. No one seems to know what assessments are given on each of my courses and we get overloaded that way. |
| Interviewer: | So if they were spread out more evenly? |
| Student 2: | That would help, but we also need less. I know that I am better than the assessments I hand in. |
| Interviewer: | Better? |
| Student 2: | Well, I am always doing the best I can in a short space of time, but never doing what I know I am really capable of. In the end, my marks will not show what I can really do. |
| Interviewer: | So would you prefer one final exam? |
| Student 2: | No way! |
| Student 1: | No way! |

practice of frequent summative assessment is already embedded. If there is no cross-curriculum agreement or university-wide policy to guide reasonable assessment practices, then academics must look to themselves to resist the dominant culture in at least some of their own work and ensure they have the freedom to assess what is genuinely valued.

## Thoughts for reflection

Barnett (1997) argued that critical thinking must lead to action and that thinking and doing then become embodied in the graduate as a 'critical being'. Critical thinking, on its own, is not enough, especially if thinking is decoupled from action. We do not, for example, accept good thinking in our politicians who then fail to carry out their pre-election promises; we might like to think that we judge them on what they achieve.

So, too, should we judge students. I would go one step further than Barnett and suggest we need to educate for a critical conscience or we undermine one of higher education's fundamental values: that students act as critic and conscience of society (Chapter 9). A critical conscience stems from caring enough about something to use one's intellect and then to act according to one's conscience. We can imagine a step-wise goal for university teaching in the following diagram:

*Figure 10.2* A model of critical thinking as critical conscience

Here critical thinking and action are integrated in the idea of a critical being. If we accept critical conscience as the ultimate purpose of a higher education then what is it that university academics need to 'add' so that students, as critical beings, achieve critical conscience? Thinking about such purposes tests the values of academic life.

## References

Barnett, R. (1997) *Higher education: a critical business*, Buckingham: Society for Research in Higher Education and Open University Press.

——(2003) *Beyond all reason: Living with ideology in the university*, Buckingham: Society for Research in Higher Education and Open University Press.

Biggs, J. & Tang, C. (2007) *Teaching for quality learning at university*, Maidenhead: McGraw Hill and Open University Press.

Bloom, B.S., Engelhart, M.D., Furst, E.J., Hill, W.H. & Krathwohl, D.R. (1956) *Taxonomy of educational objectives: The classification of educational goals. Handbook 1: Cognitive domain*, New York: David McKay.

Facione, P.A. (1990) *Critical thinking: A statement of expert consensus for purposes of educational assessment and instruction. Research findings and recommendations*, Newark, NJ: American Philosophical Association.

Krathwohl, D.R. (2002) A revision of Bloom's taxonomy: An overview, *Theory into Practice*, 41(4), 212–18.

Pascarella, E.T. & Terenzini, P.T. (1991) *How college affects students: Findings and insights from twenty years of research*, San Francisco, CA: Jossey-Bass.

Trotter, E. (2006) Student perceptions of continuous summative assessment, *Assessment and Evaluation in Higher Education*, 31(5), 505–21.

Wass, R., Harland, T. & Mercer, A. (2011) Scaffolding critical thinking in the zone of proximal development, *Higher Education Research and Development*, 30(3), 317–28.

## Further reading

Brookfield, S.D. (1987) *Developing critical thinkers: Challenging adults to explore alternative ways of thinking and acting*, San Francisco: Jossey-Bass.
Postman, N. & Weingartner, C. (1969) *Teaching as a subversive activity*, New York: Dell Publishing Co.

# Field note 10
## Pockets of resistance

When I look across my university I find examples of courses that stand out in my mind as exceptional in some way. As an academic developer I have been privileged to work on the periphery of many such programmes and what I find particularly interesting is that they have certain characteristics in common. They tend to:

1 consist of small local events that are often kept private from colleagues;
2 be grounded in the liberal educational ideal of higher education;
3 require large investments of time and energy for students and teachers;
4 have a transformational impact on students;
5 be constantly under threat.

What I think happens is that many academics are making the most of limited opportunities to teach in quite hostile conditions. Their values are often denied across the full range of their teaching responsibilities so they look for spaces where they can realize what they believe to be a good educational experience for students and satisfy their teaching needs. For various reasons, such as high student numbers, compulsory courses, teaching in large teams, shortage of time and competing demands, they cannot do this in all their teaching. So they concentrate effort in courses that I have come to think of as providing 'pockets of resistance' that serve to keep the liberal educational ideal alive and well. The reason I use the word resistance is that these courses tend to be under threat because others see them as too costly, in terms of both teacher and student effort and financial investment. The liberal educational ideal is founded on the critical traditions of higher education and experiences that support the self-actualization of the learner. Bill Readings (1996) observes that we are losing this tradition and students no longer think of themselves as embarking on a long voyage of self-discovery.

Readings, B. (1996) The university in ruins, Cambridge, MA: Harvard University Press.

# Index

Note: page numbers in **bold** refer to figures and tables

academic freedom 89, 90, 96, 100
academic work 19, 84–94,
action research 12, **13**, 18
affective domain 47, 54, 112
Angelo, T. 17, 38, 64
approaches to learning 7, 46,
    59–62, science **72**
approach to teaching 46
assessment 110–115; diagnostic 63;
    formative 110; purposes of 112;
    summative 114, 115; uncritical,
    **113**; students' views **115**
Ausubel, D. 37, 38; advance
    organizer 37

Barnett, R. 100–1, 106, 113, 116
Bloom's Taxonomy **111**, 112
Bligh, D. 33, 37
Boyer, E. 12–14
Brookfield, S. 47, 54, 117
Bruner, J. 7, 62, 63

Classroom assessment techniques
    (CATs), 17, 38, 64
community of inquiry 48, 52, 54
continuum of inquiry **63**
constructivism 58, 62–6
constructivist alignment 59–60
Cross, P. 17, 38, 64
critic and conscience 98–100, **116**;
    critical thinking 59, 106–116;
    assessment of 112; definitions
    108–9; disposition 109; quiz **107**

data, multiple sources 16
Dewey, J. 51, 100
digital 54; native 70–1
discussion 18, 28; as an approach to
    teaching 46–57

Education Act (NZ) 99, 100
Elton, L. 22, 82
Engagement 48, 52, 54; model **43**
engaging students, 34
evidence-based practice 12, 24
exam 44, 113, 114

field note 17
fragile children 74
Furedi, F. 74

group work 50–51

higher-order learning 47, 52
human capital 69, 70

induction 84, **88**, 89
inquiry 1,12,18; 29; critical 19:
    community of 48, 52, 54; forms
    of 18; made public; mutual 28;
    see also Action Research Cycle
internet 65, 71, 72

knowledge 2, 11; dissemination 9,
    33, 39, 96; hierarchy 18, 22; in
    discussion 47; tacit 58, 102;
    economy 69, 101; from research,

81; *see also* Scholarship of Teaching and Learning and Critical Thinking

learning: about teaching Chapter 1; *see also* approaches to; constructivism; problem-based
lecture 32; performance 34, 43, 45
lecturing Chapter 3; engagement 43
liberal education 9, 49, 100, 101, 105

medium is the message 41, 71
mentor groups 77, 79
mentoring 3, 8, 20, 77, 88
mission statements 15, 96, 99, 101

neoliberal 8, 87, 101, 102
Net generation 70
new academic 74, 84, 90, 98, 106; and research Chapter 7
New Zealand 2, 8, 9, 89, 97; Education Act 99–100

objectives 48, 49, 61, 95, 111; for learning 37, 107, 111; for discussion 47 Fig 4.1
outcomes 9, 96; education 59; of research 18; for learning 16, 61, 112

Patton, M.Q. 19
PBL *see* problem-based learning
peer review Chapter 2, 67
power 89, 91
PowerPoint 6, 16, 30, 36, 39–41, 70
Preskill, S. 47
problem-based learning 42,65
professional formation 1
purposes 1, **96**, 116; fit for 111; of research and teaching 80; of a higher education 9; Chapter 9

questioning Chapter 4; probe 50, 53; right answer 51, 53; techniques **53**; wait time 53

reflective practice 18, 19
research for learning Chapter 1

research and teaching 79–81
research into teaching 17
Rowland, S. 20

scaffolding 63–4
Scholarship of teaching and learning (SoTL) 12–18
society 86, 90, 95–103
service 3, 11, 13, 84, 90, 98, 100
stakeholder views 9. 96, 102
standards 9, 38, 70, 74, 99, 102, 111
Stenhouse, L. 12
students as customers 35, 68; subject 35, 42, 44, 47, 49, 51, 58, 61, 74; and critical thinking, Chapter 10; and learning 61, 65, 98; and research 77, 80; of one's own teaching 79; students views 61

teaching characteristics 12, **14**, 15
teaching load 85, 88; *see also* workload
teaching methods 42, 46, 59, 110; discussion workshop 50–1
technology 8, 36, 41–4, 68, 70–74
time management 84

university education 64, 97; positive impact on learning 64, **97**; negative impact on learning **97**

values 47–49, 112, 116 Chapter 9; formation 47, 49, 53; value commitment 2, 82, 116
valuing teaching 65
Vygotsky, L. 62

Western liberal system 9, 101, 116
workload 35, 36, 79; model 85
writing 4, 40, 73, 79, 82; for discussion 50, 54; reflective 28, 98; and thinking 109

Zone of Current Development **63**
Zone of Proximal Development 62, **63**